Father Mark O'Keeffe RAChD

David Rowlands 1999

14

IRISH GUARDS

THE FIRST HUNDRED YEARS 1900–2000

To Dick Farnsworth
with best wishes
From the Irish Guards
Quis Separabit

Brian O'Connor
Lieutenant Colonel
Regimental Adjutant

1 April 2009

IRISH GUARDS

THE FIRST HUNDRED YEARS 1900–2000

Introduction by
Her Majesty Queen Elizabeth The Queen Mother

Foreword by
General His Royal Highness the Grand Duke of Luxembourg KG
Colonel, Irish Guards

Dedicated to all who have served in the Irish Guards

SPELLMOUNT PUBLISHERS
STAPLEHURST

British Library Cataloguing in Publication Data:
A catalogue record for this book is available from the British Library

Copyright © Headquarters, Irish Guards 2000

ISBN 1-86227-069-4

First Published in the UK in 2000 by
Spellmount Limited
The Old Rectory
Staplehurst
Kent TN12 0AZ

1 3 5 7 9 8 6 4 2

Designed and produced by Pardoe Blacker Publishing Limited

Printed in Italy

CONTENTS

Endpapers:
Top – Irish Guards in Prayer before Battle, 1916
by Caton Woodville.
Bottom – Father Mark O'Keefe holding a Church
Parade for the Irish Guards in Petrovec, Macedonia,
June 1999, immediately before deployment to Kosovo.
(© David Rowlands 2000)

For 32 years I have had the great pleasure of presenting Shamrock to the Irish Guards on St Patrick's Day.

This gift has enabled me to forge a link with the Regiment which I greatly cherish, and wherever they are serving, at home or abroad, my heart and best wishes will go with them.

Elizabeth R

Her Majesty Queen Elizabeth The Queen Mother

FOREWORD

It is with great pride that I commend this story of the first hundred years of the Irish Guards. I had the privilege of serving as an officer in the Regiment during the Second World War. Since 1984 I have been the Colonel of the Regiment. Therefore I have had the opportunity for over 50 years to know The Micks at war and in peacetime.

This book records the life of the Regiment since its formation by Queen Victoria to commemorate the bravery of her Irish soldiers in South Africa. Those unique Irish characteristics of exuberance and relish for a good fight, loyalty, kindness, courage and humour have been our heritage. As you turn the pages these traits are evident: traits honed by the traditions, training and standards of the Household Division and coupled with that unquantifiable Mick spirit.

I have found the book similar to a family scrapbook, which indeed is very appropriate as this is essentially the story of a family Regiment. Formal group photographs are interspersed with the less discreet snap, happy occasions mingle with the less felicitous, moments of great honour merge with the comical, press cuttings jostle with sketches, heroes rub shoulders with scallywags, pomp and ceremony alternate with the horror and carnage of war. Put together they show how the Regiment has maintained its ethos and character throughout the challenges and changes of the past century.

I acknowledge with deep gratitude the contributions of many members of the Regiment, both retired and serving, who have made this book possible.

The Irish Guards have served with distinction for one hundred years. This book is a memorial to those who made the Irish Guards what they are today – they who served before and often sacrificed their lives in the service of this country. It should inspire us and succeeding generations to maintain the spirit and qualities of the Regiment.

Quis Separabit

Jean

Thank you for the Bird Book!

Wencestas de Nassau. Grand son of Jean

General His Royal Highness The Grand Duke of Luxembourg KG
Colonel, Irish Guards

The Irish Guards.

We're not so old in the Army List,
    But we're not so young at our trade
For we had the honour at Fontenoy
    Of meeting the Guards' Brigade.
'Twas Lally, Dillon, Bulkeley, Clare
    And Lee that led us then —
And, after a hundred and seventy years,
    We're fighting for France again!

        Old days! The Wild Geese are flighting
            Head to the storm as they faced it before.
        For where there are Irish there's bound to be fighting
            And when there's no fighting, it's Ireland no more!
                Ireland no more!

The fashion's all for khaki now,
    But once through France we went
Full-dressed in scarlet Army cloth
    The English — left at Ghent!
They're fighting on our side to-day
    But, before they changed their clothes,
The half of Europe knew our forms,
    As all of Ireland knows!

        Old days! The Wild Geese are flying
            Head to the storm as they faced it before.
        For, where there are Irish there's memory undying,
            And when we forget, it is Ireland no more!
                Ireland no more!

From Barry Wood to Gouzeaucourt
    From Boyne to Pilkem Ridge,
The ancient years return no more
    Non water under the bridge.
But the bridge it stands and the water runs
    As red as yesterday,
And the Irish go to the sound of the guns
    Like salmon to the sea!

        Old days! The Wild Geese are ranging
            Head to the storm as they faced it before.
        For where there are Irish the heart is unchanging
            And when it is changed, it is Ireland no more!
                Ireland no more!

We're not so old in the Army List
    But we're not so new in the ring,
For we carried our packs with Marshall Saxe
    When Lows was our King!
But Douglas Haig's our Marshall now
    And we're King George's men
And — after a hundred and seventy years —
    We're fighting for France again!

        Ah France! Did we stand by you
            When life was made splendid with gifts and rewards?
        Ah France! And will we deny you
            In the hour of your agony, Mother of Swords!
        Old days! The Wild Geese are flighting
            Head to the storm as they faced it before.
        For where there are Irish there's loving and fighting
            And, when we stop either, it's Ireland no more!
                Ireland no more!

March. 17. 1918.

Rudyard Kipling

Rudyard Kipling's close involvement with the Irish Guards stems from the death of his only son when serving with the 2nd Battalion in Loos in 1915. A young man of infinite charm and merit, known as 'the Joker', his parents never fully recovered from his death.

In his memory Kipling wrote his incomparable two volume history of the Irish Guards in the Great War, many extracts from which appear in the following pages.

28 February 1900
Letter to the Editor of 'The Times'
Sir,

May I venture to suggest, through you, to the authorities within whose province it may come, that now is a most opportune time to recognise the distinguished valour of our Irish soldiers who, in the Inniskilling Fusiliers, the Dublin Fusiliers and the Connaught Rangers, have shown to the world such conspicuous bravery in the many recent battles which they have fought with such brilliant dash and daring throughout our South Africa War. Is there not one mark of distinction and honour that can be conferred upon them and their country which belongs to Scotchmen and Englishmen, but is witheld from them? There are Scotch Guards and English Guards – why not add to the roll of glory a regiment of Irish Guards?

I am, Sir,
Your obedient Servant,
Cumming Macdona,
House of Commons

3 March 1900
From The Queen's Private Secretary in reply to the Secretary of State for War.
Windsor Castle,
My Dear Lord Lansdowne,

By a curious coincidence The Queen has during the past week been seriously considering the question of a Regiment of Irish Guards, thinking that the present was an opportunity for its creation. Therefore I am glad to be able to tell you that The Queen entirely approves of the idea ... Her Majesty asked the Duke of Connaught to speak to the Commander in Chief on the subject and hope that you will therefore find that Lord Wolseley is already in possession of Her Majesty's views.

Yours very truly,
(signed) Arthur Bigge

Army Order 77
1 April 1900
Formation of Regiment of Irish Foot Guards
Her Majesty The Queen, having deemed it desirable to commemorate the bravery shown by the Irish regiments in the recent operations in South Africa, has been graciously pleased to command that an Irish Regiment of Foot Guards be formed.

This regiment will be designated the 'Irish Guards'.

The House of Commons, 1 April 1900
After the Under Secretary of State for War had announced the formation of a fourth Regiment of Foot Guards to be called the Irish Guards, an Irish MP rose to his feet. It was a great day for Ireland and he waxed lyrical:

'And Mr Speaker, Sir,' he pronounced in ringing tones, 'may I assure your Honour that as fine a heart will beat under the tunic of an Irish Guard as under the kilt of a Gordon Highlander.'

CHAPTER ONE

1900-1914

THE EARLY YEARS

The Irish Guards were raised in April 1900 to commemorate the bravery of the Irish regiments in South Africa in the years 1899 and 1900.

The first British troops in action were a Mounted Infantry section of the Royal Dublin Fusiliers. Irish regiments held the ring before reinforcements arrived and they continued to feature prominently in the campaign as it developed. County Tipperary, with one of the lowest densities of population in the British Isles, had the highest number of Victoria Cross winners.

The campaign in South Africa was characterised by great bravery, and a lack of awareness of tactical changes which new and better weapons necessitated. The masterly fieldcraft of the Boers, coupled with out of date British tactics, brought a rash of humiliating defeats on the British in 1899. Through all this shone the dash and extraordinary courage of the Irish soldier.

This was brought to the attention of Queen Victoria. Simultaneously a number of letters in *The Times* suggested the formation of a Regiment of Irish Guards. So it came about that on 1 April 1900, the Fourth, or Irish Regiment of Foot Guards was born.

12 June 1901. Distribution of South African War Medals by Edward VII. This was the first royal Guard of Honour found by the Irish Guards, and the first official appearance of the Regimental Band. In the photograph The King has just arrived on Horse Guards and is being greeted by a Royal salute but with no Colour available to be lowered.

Applications to join the regiment started at once. C/Sjt Conroy of the Munster Fusiliers was awarded regimental number 1. Irishmen serving in the other regiments of the Brigade of Guards were encouraged to transfer. Very soon that unique blend between the Brigade discipline and the Irishman's wit began to brew the magic that matured into a regiment of infinite daring, ever stylish and brave, and always ready to laugh. Thus, when the call came for Mounted Infantry to go to the war in South Africa there were volunteers a-plenty. The resulting composite companies were instantly nicknamed the Aldershot Mounted Foot. This attitude of healthy irreverence permeated all that went on, behind the formidable wax moustaches of the era. The DSOs awarded to Lord Herbert Montagu-Douglas-Scott and Lord Settrington who served on the staff were instantly christened the 'Dukes' Sons Only'. Rumour, indeed, had it that the delicate shade of St Patrick's blue that Lady Settrington dyed her husband's white Grenadier plume on his transfer to the Irish Guards matched her dainty silken unmentionables.

Meanwhile, the Regiment began to appear in public to the intense interest of the press. Fine men of superb physique, they had good reason to be proud to belong to the most fashionable regiment and one they held to be without question not only the most novel but assuredly the best.

Opposite: **Field Marshal Frederick Sleigh Earl Roberts of Kandahar, Pretoria and Waterford** VC, KG, KP, GCB, GCSI, GCIE. Lord Roberts was Commander-in-Chief in South Africa. He ordered his ADCs to transfer to the new regiment, both of whom were on the first King's Guard mounted by the Regiment. Lord Roberts was in South Africa when the Regiment was formed, so he was not formally appointed Colonel of the Regiment until 17 October 1900. 'Bobs' (Lord Roberts) was the hero of the hour, his son having been killed earning a posthumous Victoria Cross at Colenso. The news reached Dublin where Lord Roberts was GOC-in-C Irish Command on the same day that he was ordered to proceed to South Africa as Commander-in-Chief. The Irish Guards, as soon as Lord Roberts was appointed Colonel, became affectionately known in his lifetime as 'Bobs' Own'.

Right: **The Original Recruiting Poster.** Note the public recognition of the bravery of the Irish Regiments.

Below: **'My Brave Irish'** – The Irish Fusiliers in South Africa, by Caton Woodville.

Capt Hubert Francis Crichton, Adjutant 19 May 1900–31 Dec 1901, formerly Grenadier Guards. Served under Kitchener at Khartoum, and was ADC to General Sir John French before the Great War. (Died of wounds received at Villers-Cottérêts, 1 Sep 1914).

Six early recruits. Note the Broderick cap did not carry a cap star, nor was a belt worn in undress uniform.

Colonel V.J. Dawson CVO, **first Regimental Lieutenant-Colonel, formerly Coldstream Guards** (3 Sep 1900–2 Sep 1905). Generations of his family had served in the Foot Guards since the Peninsular War. As a young man he lived at 16 Charles Street, Mayfair, later to become the Guards Club. He served in the Guards Camel Regiment in the Nile expedition in 1884 and left splendid photographs of that time. He had been Commanding Officer of the newly raised 3rd Battalion Coldstream Guards, so was ideally suited to the appointment as first Regimental Lieutenant-Colonel. He was very well known in both Ireland and England and was a personal friend of The King.

Ptes White and Jordan, Pirbright 1900. Note the old stand at ease position, and the fact that no regimental buckles have yet been produced for the waist belts, so the universal royal crest pattern is in use. What was called the Slade Wallace buff equipment remained for ceremonial use until the outbreak of war in 1939.

First Superintending Clerk at Regimental Headquarters Serjeant Major Dean. Note that he wears the crown as a badge of rank (Warrant Officer Class II was not introduced until 1914).

Queen Victoria's Funeral. The Irish Guards marching detachment at Paddington Station. Note the carriage of arms reversed, and the Slade Wallace equipment. For this occasion the Regiment produced its first ever detatchment of street liners.

The first King's Guard furnished by His Majesty's new regiment of Irish Guards from Chelsea Barracks, Sunday 3 March 1901. When this photograph was taken the war was still in progress in South Africa and medals had not yet been presented nor had the Regiment's Colours. Opinions, then as now, differed on the success of the Guard, one commentator saying: 'The men presented a motley appearance as the uniforms were by no means complete, and certain items of ceremonial equipment were still awaiting issue.'

Officers and Serjeants of the first King's Guard.
Seated L–R: Capt H.F. Crichton (formerly Grenadier Guards' Adjutant). (Note a captain then wore two stars.) Lt Lord Herbert Montagu-Douglas-Scott (lieutenants wore one star) and Lt Lord Settrington (missing in action 13 Apr 1918); Major G.C. Nugent (formerly Grenadier Guards, killed as Major-General, 31 May 1915); 2/Lt W. Brookes, Ensign with no colour belt, and no badge of rank as was the custom for ensigns (killed 7 Oct 1914); and 2/Lt Lord Kingston (wounded 1 Nov 1914). *Standing:* RSM C.A. Burt; C/Sjt Loughran; Sjt Brennan; Sjt Roberts; L/Sjt Brown; D/Sjt Baylis (a Colour Serjeant, wearing a Warrant Officer's tunic).

On 1 March 1900 it had been authorised, as a mark of appreciation of the great gallantry of the Irish Regiments in South Africa, that the Shamrock might be worn on St Patrick's Day, 17 March, each year.

A fortnight after the Regiment's first Guard, on St Patrick's Day 1901, the Battalion was formed up in Chelsea Barracks having just returned from church where they had worn the Shamrock just presented by the Regiment. An orderly from the Palace marched up to the Commanding Officer, Lt-Col R.J. Cooper MVO, bearing a number of boxes. These contained Shamrock, a present from Queen Alexandra herself to the new regiment. Immediately the previous Shamrock was replaced by the royal gift. So commenced an especially treasured tradition which sets the seal on the St Patrick's Day parade which each year repeats its own unique brand of intimacy and informal formality – and not a little poignancy.

The late Colonel Vandeleur.

Lieutenant-Colonel CECIL FOSTER SEYMOUR VANDELEUR, of the Irish Guards (of whose sad but glorious death a brief notice was given in our September issue), greatly distinguished himself in other parts of Africa. He was the eldest son of Mr. HECTOR STEWART VANDELEUR, of Kilrush House, County CLARE, and Cahircon, ENNIS, in the same county, and of 72, Cadogan Square, LONDON, who last year was appointed Lord Lieutenant for County CLARE,

Above: **Colonel Seymour Vandeleur** DSO, formerly Scots Guards, killed in South Africa.

Below: **1st Company Guards Mounted Infantry; Irish Guards contingent**. Here the Irish Guards contingent in tunics, medals, Broderick caps (with stars) and khaki breeches with puttees, and leather bandoliers pose at Aldershot with Lord Herbert Scott and Major (later General Sir Alexander) Godley. The latter was Baden-Powell's right hand man at the siege of Mafeking, where Captain (later Brigadier General) E.C. FitzClarence won the Victoria Cross.

No 1 Guards Mounted Infantry Company, in South Africa.

Officers of the Guards Mounted Infantry Companies left for South Africa in November 1901.
L–R: Lt B.G. Van de Wever Scots Guards, 2/Lt J.H.J. Phillips Coldstream Guards, Lt the Hon C.M.B. Ponsonby, Lt H.F. Ward Irish Guards and Capt J. Ponsonby Coldstream Guards. The head dress, uniquely, incorporated the coloured band worn on the soldier's Broderick and forage caps.

The first Regimental Serjeant Major, C.A. Burt, photographed at the Tower of London. Serjeant Major Burt transferred to the Regiment from the Scots Guards. He had served in Ashanti and South Africa.

St Patrick's Day, Tower of London, 1902. The first occasion when the newly approved Regimental marches were played on St Patrick's Day. After the parade things became more informal. Here the Bigophone Band pose for the camera that afternoon.

Tower of London, 1902. The Officers, 1st Battalion Irish Guards.

Battalion football team. Lt-Col R.J. Cooper MVO, the first Commanding Officer, at the Tower of London, 1902. Lt-Col Cooper, from Colooney, Co. Sligo, served with 2nd Battalion Grenadier Guards in the Egyptian War of 1882. Note the shin pads. Where is the eleventh player?

Below: **Warrant Officer and Staff Serjeants, Tower of London 1902.** Capt Crichton and Serjeant Major Burt are flanked by the Battalion staff (hence the expression staff serjeant). They carry a staff cane bearing the regimental insignia.

The first Bandmaster 1902, Bandmaster C.H. Hassel, before Directors of Music were introduced. Chosen from over one hundred applicants, he had enlisted at the age of 12 into the old 95th Foot (2nd Battalion The Sherwood Foresters), and then became Bandmaster 4th Battalion The King's Royal Rifle Corps. Promoted Director of Music in 1919, Capt Hassel retired in March 1929, and was awarded the OBE. Over sixty years later, Bandsmen in the Foot Guards were, at the request of Lt-Col 'Jigs' Jaeger, re-styled formally as Musicians.

The Regimental Band in 1902, 43 strong. Photographed at Wellington Barracks.

Painting of the distribution of South African War Medals on Horse Guards Parade. Queen Alexandra (who had previously presented the Shamrock for the first time that spring) can be seen on The King's right, in Full Court Mourning after the death of Queen Victoria. (Royal Archives. By gracious permission of HM The Queen).

Opposite: **Muster Roll,** incorrectly gives a battle honour for South Africa. Produced after the presentation of colours and probably after 4 Oct 1902 when the Mounted Infantry returned. The draughtsman was ex-Sjt Hicks, a Grenadier Crimean veteran.

Battalion Swimming Team, Chelsea Barracks, *c.*1903.
Capt R.C.A. McCalmont (Adjutant 1 Jan 1904–31 Dec
1906, left, with polished boots and frock coat).
Standing second from right: 552 C/Sjt Arthur Munns
DCM, (killed 1st Ypres, 17 Nov 1914). Standing, right,
in uniform, Serjeant Major Baylis.

Change of Quarters, approaching Aldershot from Farnborough. Note full change of Quarter Order, including black leather anklets.

Settling in. 1st Battalion Irish Guards having just arrived at Oudenarde Barracks, Aldershot. QM Fowles on the square with sheaf of papers.

Brian Boru and Handler (photographed at Aldershot in 1906). *The Military Mail* reported in May 1902: 'The Irish Wolfhound Club has recently offered to make the Irish Guards a novel and appropriate presentation in the shape of a young Irish wolfhound as a regimental pet.'

Brian Boru painted by Heywood Hardy, one of a collection of portraits of wolfhounds which hang in the Officers' Mess.

Battalion Tug of War Team, Aldershot, c.1903. Left in plain clothes Major G.C. Nugent (Commanding Officer 1st Battalion 1908, Regimental Lt-Col 1909, killed 1915 commanding 5 London Brigade). Centre D/Sjt Hudson DCM (wearing no belt or sword), who won his medal in South Africa with the Mounted Infantry, the Regiment's first decoration, and a bar to his DCM when serving with the Irish Fusiliers at Salonika in the Great War.

Barrack Room, Christmas 1903, Oudenarde Barracks, Aldershot. Whilst at Aldershot the Battalion was under command of the GOC Aldershot, Lt General Sir Horace Lockwood Smith-Dorrien, whose name every man had to know. In addition to his later fame in the Great War, this officer had the distinction of being one of the very few survivors from the Zulu massacre at Isandlwana in 1879, at the time of Rorke's Drift.

No 8 Company's Barrack Room, Oudenarde Barracks, Aldershot, 1904. The trestle tables are ready for a meal, since no mess room had been introduced and meals were collected from the cook house (hence 'come to the cook house door boys'). Beneath each folded bed is at least one soldier's box. The slouch hats are the equivalent of today's combat cap. The small blue plume worn in these hats was later adopted as the pipers' hackle.

St Patrick's Day, Aldershot 1906. Shamrock is being distributed round the companies of the Battalion which are drawn up in mass. The Regimental Wolfhound, Brian Boru, is visible on the left.

In 1906 the Army at Home undertook major manoeuvres. As part of this activity the Irish Guards were involved in a complicated amphibious landing at Southend. Here No 8 Company complete with slouch hats and Slade Wallace equipment goes ashore from lighters.

Officers' Mess Cart on manoeuvres, 1906.

Pay Sjts 1st Battalion Aldershot, 1906. Each company had a Pay Serjeant, who would now be the CQMS. The Colour Serjeant was the equivalent of the Company Serjeant Major. Silver topped Malacca canes were carried by senior ranks.

The Colours, 1910. *Left:* **Pte FitzGerald.** *Centre:* **D/Sjt Bracken.** *Right:* **Pte Gilliland.** The Regimental Colour on the right carries the No 1 Company badge. Originally intended to bear the Royal Cypher, the design VR was submitted to King Edward VII, who wanted his cypher included as well.

Field Marshal Lord Roberts, first Colonel of the Irish Guards, mounted at
Buckingham Palace for The King's Birthday parade 1913. This photograph was taken
specially for personal distribution. Lord Roberts is wearing the sash and star of the
Order of St Patrick. His black riding boots are worn outside his overalls as was
customary at the time.

The Corps of Drums 1911–1912, HM Tower of London.
34 strong, 8 side drummers (including the boys).
Centre: Capt & Adjutant The Hon Jack (Hepburn-Scott-) Trefusis (Adjutant 2 Dec 1909–1 Jun 1913) whose letters and war diaries are some of the most vivid ever written.

Wearing khaki for the first time in London. An early instance of duties in aid of the Civil Power. An Irish Guards sentry on duty, complete with bearskin cap, during the railway strike of 1911, at Grosvenor Road railway station.

Presentation of the second stand of Colours, Buckingham
Palace, 28 June 1913, by HM King George V.

Boxing Team, 1910–1911, Chelsea Barracks. Capt James Fowles, the first Quartermaster, affectionately known to all as 'Ginger' was an enthusiast in all he did. He was no inconsiderable performer in the ring himself and the real instigator of Army boxing. He also set up the 'Shamrock Minstrel Troupe' which featured large in concerts of the day.

Back Row Standing L–R: Pte Dan 'The Pounder' Voyles, Household Brigade and Army and Navy Heavyweight Champion; Pte Donovan, Light Heavyweight Champion, Household Brigade; Pat O' Keeffe, Instructor and Middleweight Champion of England. *Front Row L–R:* Pte P. McEnroy, Finalist Army and Navy Championship; Capt and QM James Fowles; RSM J. Myles; Pte A. Sinclair, Welterweight Champion Household Brigade.

Opposite page:
Testament to Capt Fowles on his retirement. Commissioned as Quartermaster to the Irish Guards from the Grenadiers on 24 May 1900, he nevertheless appeared in his previous role some days later as Regimental Serjeant Major of the 1st Battalion Grenadier Guards providing the Escort to the Colour.

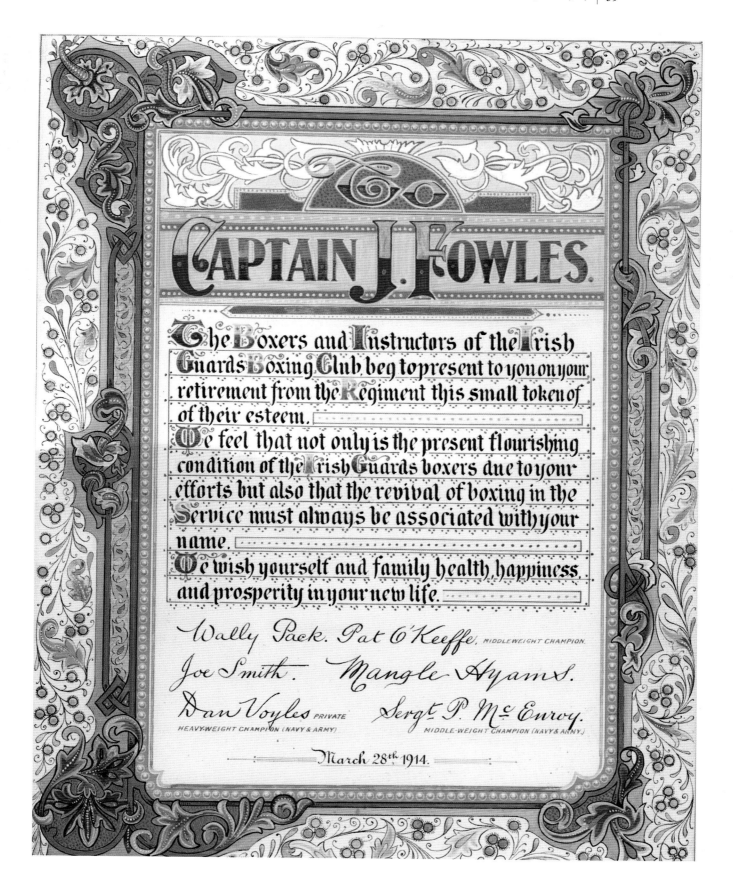

Irish Guards stretcher bearers on duck boards
near Ayette/St Leger during the German
Offensive, March 1918.

CHAPTER TWO

1914–1918

THE GREAT WAR

War was declared at noon on 4 August 1914. Since dawn that day the boat trains from Ireland had been arriving in London bringing to Wellington Barracks, the home of 1st Battalion Irish Guards, reservists who, anticipating their summons and determined not to miss the 'excitement', had boarded the Mail Boats the previous evening. Everyone confidently predicted it would all be over by Christmas.

Four years and three months later, having earned four Victoria Crosses, and after the Regiment had sustained 7,488 casualties (2,349 killed) out of 9,633 all ranks engaged, the 'War to end Wars' came to its exhausted, bloody conclusion. The Victory Medal awarded to each of the survivors was inscribed 'The Great War for Civilisation 1914–1919'.

The Great War brought to an end an era. Its scale (more than four hundred medals for distinguished service or bravery were hard earned by Irish Guardsmen) and the slaughter have engraved images of the savagery and filth of trench warfare in the nation's memory. To remind us, there are, of course, the official accounts, carefully written up after the event. The Regimental Archives is also a priceless source of magnificent photographic cover of much of the Great War. Of the most bloody and tragic parts, however, we only have word pictures in vivid letters and deeply moving dog-eared, smudged, personal trench diaries.

The six stages, as the Regiment saw the Great War, were:

THE FIRST STAGE, 1914. The excitement of mobilization; the long dusty Retreat from Mons to near Paris; confused, fluid fighting in woods; snipers and the first simple trenches; the sacrifice at First Ypres saved the Channel Ports. A sense of newness and unreality.

THE SECOND STAGE, 1915. Hold the line.

Stroke and counter stroke in France and Belgium. First use of gas. The Regiment's first Victoria Cross awarded to L/Cpl Michael O'Leary. 2nd Battalion Irish Guards formed 15 July 1915. The Guards Division formed August 1915 under Lord Cavan.

THE THIRD STAGE, 1916. The Somme.

The Battle of the Somme was designed to take pressure off the French who were struggling to hold Verdun. In this the British effort succeeded, at huge cost.

THE FOURTH STAGE, 1917. The Hindenburg Line, Passchendaele and Cambrai.

The cumulative strain of the Somme and Verdun forced the Germans to withdraw some 15 miles to a prepared defensive line, the Hindenburg Line. The next British offensive was to have been at Arras, but the sudden German withdrawal altered the plans.

Such had been the pressure on the French too, that French mutinies broke out. To give time to restore the French Army, a huge British offensive was rushed ahead, at Ypres. Criticised for being ill-timed on account of the rains, the timing was unavoidable if the French armies were to have a chance to recover. This hideous battle, ever since associated with mud and blood, became known as Passchendaele, during which both L/Sjt Moyney and Pte Woodcock won the Victoria Cross.

After Passchendaele the Regiment took part in the costly Cambrai offensive which, as so often, had promised so much.

What it remembered was hell in Bourlon Wood.

THE FIFTH STAGE, January–July 1918. The German Offensive.

The collapse of Russia in the revolution of 1917 enabled German strength on the Western Front to increase by one third. Sapped by the losses at Passchendaele, on the British side every brigade had effectively lost one of its four Battalions, which had not been fully replaced. The Germans broke through, re-capturing every yard of all the Somme gains. An acute crisis developed as the Germans poured through in huge numbers dangerously close to the Channel ports. There were no British reserves. The 2nd Battalion (in 4th Guards Brigade) in an heroic last ditch effort at Hazebrouck, held the German onrush, saved France, and finished off the fighting capability of 4th Guards Brigade for the rest of the War.

THE SIXTH STAGE, July–November 1918. Advance to Victory: Canal du Nord, Hindenburg Line.

A British offensive opened on 8 August 1918 and continued to the Armistice. During this phase Lt (Acting Lt-Col) Neville Marshall won a posthumous Victoria Cross whilst commanding a Battalion of the Lancashire Fusiliers. The Irish Guards finished at Maubeuge (near Mons, almost where they had started in 1914), arriving on 9 November 1918. Here they heard of the Armistice.

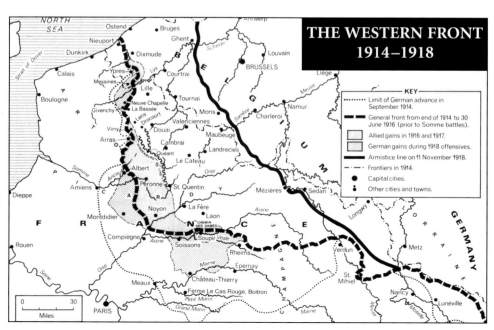

Officers of the 1st Battalion Irish Guards, Wellington Barracks, August 1914, prior to departure for the British Expeditionary Force (BEF), France.
L–R: Lt the Hon H.G. Hugo Gough (wounded October 1914), 2/Lt E.C. Stafford-King-Harman (killed 6 November 1914 near Ypres), Capt the Hon Tom Vesey (No 3 Company; wounded October 1914), Lt the Hon H.R. Alexander (wounded 1 November 1914) the future Field Marshal, Lt J.S.N. FitzGerald (No 2 Company, twice decorated, served throughout the war without a scratch from August 1914 to 11 November 1918, and then went to Russia). *Seated:* Lt C.A. Walker (No 1 Company).

'*Sunday 9 August 1914. Church Parade. In afternoon the Battalion went on a route march – in full war kit (minus ammunition) … marched through Trafalgar Square etc. Crowds cheering the whole time. Halted at Regent's Park, and returned via Hyde Park, Constitution Hill*'. Diary of 2587 Pte Kilcoin, a reservist who had just been recalled.

Irish Guards off to the War, 1914. Here the 1st Battalion Irish Guards (a total of 32 Officers and 1,100 rank and file of which 98% were Irish and 90% Roman Catholic) marches out of the West Gate of Wellington Barracks early on 12 August 1914, heading for Nine Elms Station and Southampton. Each detachment was played off by the Regimental Band, according to Kipling. This photograph bears this out, since the drum is being carried. The Officer is Major H.A. Herbert-Stepney (known in the Regiment as 'Spud') who is leading No 2 Company. When the Commanding Officer and Second in Command both became casualties on 1 September 1914, as the only major he took temporary command for eighteen hectic days and was killed on 6 November 1914 near Ypres.

Sjt P. Gallacher marches out like he did in 1914. Wounded at 1st Ypres in November 1914, he recovered in time to go to France again when the 2nd Battalion went in 1915. He worked in the Shoemaker's Shop, and became the Master Shoemaker.

THE FIRST STAGE, 1914

After the excitement of mobilization and painstaking preparation, 1st Battalion Irish Guards sailed for France and landed at Le Havre. After a long rail journey they arrived at Wassigny, and next morning marched north to head off the anticipated German advance near Mons. No sooner had they approached the Belgian border than it became necessary to withdraw rapidly to conform with the rest of the British Expeditionary Force which was already in danger of being outflanked by the Germans. Thus, unheroically, began the Retreat from Mons (always referred to by veterans as the 'Retirement from Mons'), a most gruelling and testing withdrawal in contact, as much a test of stamina and discipline as anything.

The first serious contact was at Landrecies where a sharp night engagement in the town was followed by further withdrawal.

The day after the Battalion distantly heard what they judged a *'battle in the direction of Le Cateau'* (Kipling), 'Lee Catoo', they called it, but were not involved. The next engagement was a Brigade withdrawal in contact in the beech woods at Villers-Cottérêts on 1 September.

Here, gallantly, 4th Guards Brigade delayed the German advance long enough to prevent the other Division in the Corps from being outflanked. There were grievous casualties, including the Commanding Officer who was killed in the Battalion's first serious action.

Landrecies, 25 August 1914. Scene of 1 Corps and 4th Guards Brigade action *'An unlovely long streeted town in closely cultivated country'* (Kipling). They blockaded the road with *'stones, tables, chairs, carts, pianos'.* One of the drums was later heard going down the main street caught on a galloping horse's hoof. (This is the main street looking south, 1998.)

The Timber Yard at Wassigny (1998). *'17th August 1914. Arrived at Wassigny (our destination) and detrained in total darkness billeted in a timber yard until daybreak. Had breakfast (bully and biscuits) – Then marched off, destination unknown.'* (Pte Kilcoin's Diary).

Left: **Le Murger Farm, near Soucy** (31 August 1914). The weary Battalion defended the farm the night before the Villers-Cottérêts action, but the Germans did not catch up, and they moved off at 2am. The farm, flattened in 1918, has been identically reconstructed and the same family still lives there.

RETREAT FROM MONS

Retreat from Mons, 1914. The woods at Villers-Cottérêts. The Battalion's first serious action was as part of a brigade retirement in contact, with confused and very gallant fighting in the woods. It was imperative to impose delay on the advancing Germans so that the remainder of the exhausted Division could snatch a few hours' rest, and re-group. The Commanding Officer of the 1st Battalion was killed in the first action of the Great War, an event which, cruelly, was repeated in Norway in 1940.

The Guards Grave at Villers-Cottérêts. Two platoons of Grenadiers fought to the last man, and led by 2/Lt Cecil, with drawn sword, they gave a final bayonet charge. Ninety-three casualties from 4th Guards Brigade (and one other) who fell on 1 September 1914 were buried by the advancing Germans in what eventually became the Guards Grave. Others, including Major Crichton, the Second in Command, are buried elsewhere. Such is the legacy of a fighting withdrawal. Rudyard Kipling, whose son John was trying to join the Irish Guards, helped Lady Violet Cecil in the search for her missing son, and visited the Guards Grave. This, coupled with the disappearance of John at the battle of Loos in 1915, was Rudyard Kipling's inspiration to become a commissioner in the new Imperial War Graves Commission.

Lt-Col the Hon George Morris, Commanding Officer 1st Battalion Irish Guards. Killed in Action 1 September 1914. Colonel Morris: *'Do you hear that? They are only doing that to frighten you'.* Unknown Private: *'If that's what they're after, Sir, they might as well stop. They succeeded with me hours ago!'* (Kipling). *'We saw him riding up and down, cheering us on, and we only knew he was wounded when we saw the blood coming from his field boot.'* (Recollections of Sjt Gallacher, Master Shoemaker, 1st Battalion).

MARNE 1914

Ferme Le Cas Rouge, Boitron. Battle of the Marne, 8 September 1914. This was the turning point when the German advance from Mons was halted just east of Paris, and the Allies began the advance northwards towards the Aisne where 1st Battalion Irish Guards crossed by pontoon on 13 September 1914. The 1st Battalion spent the night in this farm after the fighting in the Boitron woods where they captured 90 German prisoners, and 6 machine-guns. They parolled the German officers and invited them to dine on chicken and red wine. The farm, undamaged in either war, remains in the hands of the same family to this day.

Fighting in the woods at Soupir. Heywood Hardy's painting shows the officers wearing their caps backwards to conceal the gold peak from snipers.

AISNE 1914

Below: **The Aisne. Le Cour de Soupir Farm.** The Connaught Rangers handed over to 1st Battalion Irish Guards (15 September 1914) and 4th Guards Brigade at Le Cour de Soupir Farm. Lt Greer's machine-gun section was lost, and here, crucially, began real trench warfare. As one private put it: *'We was like fleas in a blanket seeing no more than the next nearest wrinkle'* (Kipling). Here too, Lt Hugo Gough, later a celebrated one armed Commanding Officer of the Reserve Battalion in the Second World War, lost his arm. *'The heavily wooded country was alive with musketry and machine-gun fire, and the distances were obscured by mist and heavy rain.'* (Kipling).

Above: **Soupir.** Capt The Hon Tom Vesey sent his daughter a postcard from Soupir, and marked the places of interest. Situated just behind the Allied line throughout the 1914–18 war, the village was extensively damaged. The Château was destroyed, but the church beside which Tom Vesey had his 'billet' survived.

Aisne. Soupir Village and Woods. September–October 1914. In these woods which form the slopes of the high Chemin des Dames were fought numerous actions by 4th Guards Brigade. The area became a long term battleground until 1918. Soupir Village today still has its church, and the gates of the Château where they acquired illicit eggs. At the time everybody was familiar with Soupir from the press because of a sensation earlier in the summer when the owner of the Château, imagining herself scandalously libelled by a Paris newspaper, had confronted the editor in his office, produced a pistol from her handbag, and shot him. The case was coming to trial when war broke out, and all were curious to know what happened. The Lady was gone by the time they arrived, and other things took their attention … (Reminiscences of Sjt Gallacher, Royal Hospital, 1981).

Lt Eric Greer and one of his Maxim gun sections, August 1914. At Soupir on 14 September 1914 '*A party of Coldstream found some 150 Germans sitting round haystacks and waving white flags. They went forward to take their surrender and were met by heavy fire at 30 yards range. Lt E.B. Greer, machine-gun officer, now brought up his two machine-guns, but was heavily fired on from cover, had all of one gun team killed or wounded and, for a while, lost one gun. He re-organised the other gun team and called for volunteers from the company nearest him to recover it.*' (Kipling).

The modern Service Dress cap worn by officers resulted from the German snipers in the Soupir woods. Up to then officers in the Foot Guards wore gold peaked khaki caps with a black band, clearly different from the khaki caps worn by Other Ranks as seen on the left.

Irish Guards Graves at Soupir. Lord Arthur Hay, Capt Hamilton Berners, and Lord Guernsey, all killed 14 September 1914.

After the bitter fighting on the Aisne, at Soupir in the Irish Guards' case, the British Army moved hastily north to prevent the Germans reaching the sea on the Belgian coast. The 1st Battalion was closely engaged in this critical battle, eventually serving in the remains of 1st Guards Brigade, which had only recently been taken over by Brigadier General Charles FitzClarence VC, their former Regimental Lieutenant Colonel. He was killed and has no known grave.

The situation was so critical that the Adjutant was sent off to Brigade Headquarters to get help. It arrived – eventually. The perilously thin line was still holding out but had suffered terrible casualties, including the Commanding Officer, Lord Ardee, wounded. On 2 November they re-organised into three under-strength companies. On the 7th they lost another Commanding Officer, Major Herbert Stepney. On the 8th they reformed into two small companies. On the 9th they could muster only four platoons. On the 18th, after further losses, they were pulled back for the last time. They were relieved by a company of 3rd Coldstream – and one company sufficed. They had entered the battle over a thousand strong. Eventually eight officers and 390 men recovered. It was so cold the water froze in their water bottles. 'Not a man fell out.'

The 1st Battalion Irish Guards' losses were close on a thousand all ranks killed, wounded or missing. The Battalion had been practically wiped out, partially rebuilt and nearly wiped out again. The remnants were exhausted in mind and body; only their morale and irrepressible humour kept them going.

The famous Christmas Truce of 1914 did not affect the much depleted Battalion. They were in the 'wet dreary' trenches, two hundred yards from the Germans, under occasional heavy bombardment. Two officers and six men were wounded on Christmas day.

Brigadier General Charles FitzClarence VC at his Brigade Headquarters, France, September 1914.

YPRES 1914-17

Warley 1914. 2/Lts Vivyan Harmsworth (wounded November 1917, MC) and John Kipling (missing Loos, 1915) joined on 15 August 1914 in car, barrack square, Warley.

Volunteers of the Royal Irish Constabulary (*'large drilled men, who were to play so solid a part in the history and glory of the Battalion'*) who arrived during Neuve Chapelle, following the correspondence between the Regiment and Neville Chamberlain, Inspector General of the Royal Irish Constabulary. Two hundred had been proposed, hundreds more volunteered.

Royal Irish Constabulary Office,

Dublin Castle,

24th. November, 1914.

Sir,

I have the honour to inform you that, as the result of representations recently made by me, the Government have approved of 200 Constables of the Royal Irish Constabulary being permitted to enlist in the Irish Guards for the period of the war. From a large number of Volunteers I have selected 200 men who are between the ages of 20 and 35, who are unmarried and are recommended by their officers as being suitable as regards physique, health, intelligence, character etc.

Provision is being made, with the sanction of the Treasury, to grant these men privileges as regards the counting of Army service for the purposes of pay and pension on the lines of those conferred on Reservists by the Irish Police Constables (Naval and Military Service) Act, 1914.

I shall be glad to hear from you regarding the following points :-

1. Should the men enlist at the Recruiting Office, Gt. Brunswick Street, Dublin, specially for the Irish Guards, and, if so, will you communicate direct with the Recruiting Officer on this point and also arrange with him to issue passes for each man to proceed to the Regimental Depot at Warley, Brentford, Essex?

2. I presume the men should wear their own plain clothes when en route to Warley and that they will receive instructions from the Recruiting Officer, Dublin, as to whom they should report themselves at Warley ?

3. Will you kindly inform me whether it will be more convenient for you if the men enlist in batches of 50 and proceed to join the Regiment ? If so, could you draw out a table showing the dates on which the batches of 50 should present themselves for enlistment in Dublin ?

I have the honour to be,

Sir,

Your obedient Servant,

Neville Chamberlain

Inspector General.

Left: **Father Gwynne in the trenches** early 1915. *L–R:* Sjt McEnroy, Sjt Bennet and Rev Fr Gwynne. Of Father John Gwynne they said: 'He was not merely a chaplain, but a man unusually beloved. He feared nothing, despised no one, betrayed no confidence and comforted every man within his reach.' He was killed on 1 November 1915 when the HQ dugout was hit. Yet another Commanding Officer, Lt-Col Gerald Madden, was mortally wounded. In the first fifteen months of the Great War 1st Battalion Irish Guards lost five Commanding Officers, of whom four were killed and one was wounded.

Right: **'Sleep is sweet, Undisturbed it is divine.'** This is reputedly 2858 Pte (later L/Cpl) Green MM.

Father Gwynne, Capt McCarthy, the Battalion's superb Medical Officer, and 2/Lt Straker examine an unexploded German shell. Straker arrived in the Battalion in time for 1st Ypres, as the new Machine-Gun officer. He was seriously wounded in April 1915.

The Germans who had so nearly captured Ypres in November 1914 needed a pause to consolidate. That pause saved the Regiment. So rapidly were the new drafts made available for the 1st Battalion, it spent little time out of action. 'Airoplane Duty' was introduced in the trenches. Freezing men were issued with woollen cardigan waistcoats, and every man received a goatskin coat. Duckboards, too, an omen of things to come, joined improvised jam tin grenades as the novelties of the season. The 1st Battalion took a supporting part in the offensive mounted by the Indian Division near Cuinchy, where there had been brick factories (an indication of the clay in the soil). Stacks of bricks stood waiting to be taken away, when war arrived. Here L/Cpl Michael O'Leary suddenly leapt to international fame when he won Ireland's first Victoria Cross of the war. His fearless dash, which captured a German machine-gun post, and dispatched several other 'Huns', somehow encapsulated all the virtues upon which the regiment prided itself.

By March 1915 the jam tin grenade had become obsolete, succeeded by the 'stick grenade of the hairbrush type'. The Mills bomb was not introduced until the autumn of 1915.

Service dress caps, incredibly, were still the normal headdress even in the trenches, until the number of head wounds eventually forced the introduction, in late 1915, of the steel helmet. A 1915 letter to Regimental Headquarters in London thanks for sausages, and asks the Regimental Adjutant to contact George Potter, the Aldershot musical instrument supplier, explaining that the next lot of flutes for the Corps of Drums should be made of seasoned wood; the last consignment had warped in the damp conditions in France. And please to send some more electric cells (batteries) for the electric torches (the Regiment priding itself on being the first to have bought some of these convenient new inventions).

Re-invigorated, the Germans opened the Second Battle of Ypres on 27 April 1915. This coincided with a British attack in the Neuve Chapelle area, the purpose of which was to capture the important Aubers Ridge. The 1st Battalion took part in the offensive in the Festubert Sector, and in a ten-day battle some six hundred yards were gained, but the breakthrough never came. In the attack on La Cour L'Avoue Farm Irish Guards losses were 18 Officers and 461 Other Ranks on 15 May 1915.

The Guards Division was formed in the summer of 1915 and the two Irish Guards Battalions, meeting for the first time, eyed each other with interest. Loos (in the flat coal mining district south of the La Bassée Canal) was the last major offensive of the year in late September 1915. It was the 2nd Battalion's baptism. Like so many other battles, Loos ended tragically and at great cost. It was also the first action of the newly created 1st Battalion Welsh Guards.

'Sleep is sweet, Undisturbed it is divine,
So lift up your feet and do not tread on mine.'

So read the commanding officer one night, on finding a man deeply asleep with his feet protruding into the fairway. He made no comment, but it was remembered with affection. Despite the horrors the Battalions took life with a philosophical calm.

Those who fought in the period from 15 August to 22 November 1914 were awarded the 1914 Star (known as the Mons Star), with a clasp showing those dates. The ribbon bore a silver rosette. The 1914 Star covered all engagements up to the end of the First Battle of Ypres.

Those who fought during the period 5 August 1914 to 31 December 1915, but who had not qualified for the 1914 Star (i.e. those who had been UNDER FIRE in France or Belgium between August and November 1914 within specified dates), were awarded the 1914–15 Star which looks almost identical, but has no clasp on the ribbon (nor rosette), and which bears a single scroll in the centre giving the dates: 1914–15.

The 1914 Star.

THE SECOND STAGE, 1915. Hold the Line

Within the lines life assumed a fearful monotony, but punctuated by moments of sheer terror. From time to time they went over the top – 'popped the parapet', they called it. The technique was the same; before zero hour – or what a German once inappropriately called 'love' hour – the barrage started. Designed to cut the enemy wire on some selected piece of ground, it was of ferocious intensity. Then came the charge, when one machine-gun against you was worth a platoon, and three a company; the consolidation phase awaiting the inevitable counter-attack and, finally, the agonising roll-call.

In these attacks a man's world was the shell-wracked horizon some few yards ahead. Under these conditions comradeship could help you carry on, but it was the discipline that got you started and kept you going. And hanging over everything was that awful pretence of not being afraid.

And it was here or hereabouts that people started to talk of 'The Guards Way', as a benchmark for perfection in all matters military, a message that pervaded the Army through the enormous number of men who rose in the ranks of the Brigade and then were commissioned in other regiments.

The brick stacks at Cuinchy under fire. This is where L/Cpl O'Leary won his Victoria Cross, February 1915. (For full citation see p. 206)

L/Cpl Michael O'Leary vc. Lady Butler painted a romanticised portrait of the first Irish Guards vc.

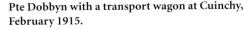

Pte Dobbyn with a transport wagon at Cuinchy, February 1915.

The discomforts of a young Officer's life in the early trenches. Vivyan Harmsworth arrived in France with a draft from Warley on 28 November 1914, just after the Battalion had been severely battered at First Ypres. Here he is shortly after arrival, not at all comfortable in Service dress.

Above: **'Irish Guards Resting', Neuve Chapelle,** March 1915. Near Aubers Ridge and La Bassée, the Battalion was involved in open attacks from inferior trenches taken over from 6th Brigade. The first very welcome ex-RIC draft arrived during Neuve Chapelle.

Meanwhile, at Warley, the training for war continued apace.

Mop fighting competition, St Patrick's Day, 1915. Training and inculcating regimental spirit went on with the 2nd (Reserve) Battalion at Warley.

Bayonet fighting competition. Training in the 2nd Battalion at Warley continued with the aim of it becoming a Service Battalion. The Bayonet fighting competition, judged by the Earl of Kerry, was an example. 'Points were awarded for speed, and for getting the bayonet through a card on the sacks.'

Machine-gun Section 2nd Battalion Irish Guards, Warley, June 1915. *Standing: Back row second from left:* Pte Legiar. *Right hand man standing on the ground:* Pte Gallagher. *Seated L–R:* Unidentified L/Cpl, Sjt Major Price, Capt Hon Tom Vesey (First Adjutant of 2nd Battalion, recovered from his wound at Soupir).

Sniper's rifle and Pte Connor DCM, April 1915, shortly before the first German chlorine gas attack during the Second Battle of Ypres. Casualties from small arms fire had been increasing because of the sodden state of the parapet. On 10 January 1915 Lt The Earl of Kingston sent up a 'telescopic-sighted' rifle. D/Sjt Bracken 'certainly' accounted for three killed and four wounded of the enemy. The War Diary, as Kipling puts it, *'mercifully blind to the dreadful years to come'* thinks *'… There should be many of these rifles used so long as the Army is sitting in trenches.'* Many of them were, and (nowadays) are so used, and this, the father of them all, is in the Guards Museum.

Recruits at Warley. As the casualties mounted in 1915 and the army expanded rapidly, equipment became scarce. Hence the RIC man wears his RIC uniform, and shoulder stars are used instead of cap stars.

Above: **A Moment of Drama,** 1 August 1915. Field Marshal Lord Kitchener's visit to 2nd and 3rd (Reserve) Battalions at Warley before the Second Battalion went to France to join the new Guards Division. In this photograph the new Colonel of the Regiment, Field Marshal Lord Kitchener (a former Sapper) looks annoyed. We now know that Lt John Kipling (known as 'the Joker') had just commented, too loudly, on a grease spot on the top of Kitchener's white cap cover. 'Anybody can see he is not a Guardsman.' Lord Kitchener, unfortunately, heard these words just as the photographer said 'Smile, please, Gentlemen ...' and the moment was captured for posterity. The witnesses were Messrs Rupert Grayson and Langrishe, each of whom also heard the remark.

Below: **Lord Kitchener's Inspection of 2nd Battalion Irish Guards (now a Service Battalion),** 13 August 1915. He expressed his belief they would be a credit to the Guards Division then being formed in France. To the Regiment's delight, the Earl of Cavan (an Irishman who was a Grenadier), who had commanded 4th Guards Brigade, assumed command of the new Guards Division. He later became the fourth Colonel of the Irish Guards.

1914–15 Star.

Above: **4th Guards Brigade leaving 2nd Divsion for the newly formed Guards Division** in which it became 1st Guards Brigade. No 4 Coy 1st Battalion, Capt Sidney FitzGerald. Pipers visible, Lt-Col G.H.C. Madden (whose son and grandson both served in the Regiment in their generations) had taken over from Lt-Col Jack Trefusis DSO (promoted Temp. Brigadier General) the previous day. This was the day 2nd Battalion left Warley for France.

Below: **2nd Battalion Irish Guards leaving Warley for France, 1915 under command of Lt-Col The Hon L. Butler.** A family regiment. The lady carrying a child is Mrs Young, wife of Capt G.E.S. Young. The baby, later Brigadier H.L.S. (Savill) Young, won the DSO with the 1st Battalion at Anzio, and his son, too, served in the Regiment in the 1960s.

LOOS

Left: **Lord Desmond FitzGerald in a shell hole,** probably taken at the Battle of Loos, September 1915. An imperturbable Adjutant, much loved, he was tragically killed in a grenade accident when training on the new Mills Bomb on the sands of Calais in March 1916.

Left: **John Kipling.** This popular, short-sighted officer was missing at Loos. Like so many others, his parents never recovered. His grave was finally identified in 1992.

Above: **In the trenches, Loos,** 1915. After the battle, the two Battalions remained in the trenches and held the section near the Hohenzollern Redoubt 'where they had many bombing encounters with the enemy' (T.H.H. Grayson).

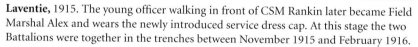

Laventie, 1915. The young officer walking in front of CSM Rankin later became Field Marshal Alex and wears the newly introduced service dress cap. At this stage the two Battalions were together in the trenches between November 1915 and February 1916.

The worst of this War is not bullets or shells, but the absence of female society that tells. For the War may through ages & ages meander, If you'll give such an ord'ly to :—
H. Alexander.

Trench visitors book: *'The worst of this war is not bullets or shells, but the absence of female society that tells.'*

In December 1915 Field Marshal Sir John French, later to become the third Colonel of the Regiment, was succeeded by Field Marshal Sir Douglas Haig as Commander-in-Chief of the British Expeditionary Force.

Rev Father S. Knapp, Battalion priest to both the 1st and 2nd Battalions. After the death of the gallant Father Gwynne, Father Knapp spoke to both Battalions. *'Those that survived that heard it say it moved all men's hearts. Mass always preceded the day's work in billets, but even on the first morning on their return from the trenches the men would make shift somehow to clean their hands and faces, and if possible to shave, before attending it, no matter what the hour'.* (Kipling). The Regimental Priest holds a treasured place in the annals of the Irish Guards. Friend to all ranks, he was also an indispensable sounding board of the mood of the Battalion to the Commanding Officer.

St Patrick's Day, 1916. 3rd (Reserve) Battalion Irish Guards, Warley. When the 2nd Battalion went to France in 1915 a 3rd (Reserve) Battalion formed at Warley. HM The King distributes Queen Alexandra's Shamrock while Queen Mary looks on. HM King George V, John Redmond MP (whose son was serving and who gave the first pipes to the Regiment; he was leader of the Irish Party in the Commons), Field Marshal Lord Kitchener who had become the second Colonel of the Regiment on the death of Lord Roberts in November 1914. He was later drowned in HMS *Hampshire* on 5 June 1916. The Regimental Lieutenant Colonel looks on.

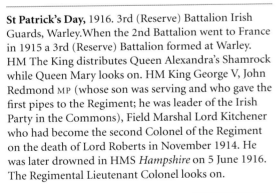

THE AFFAIR OF GINCHY.

Irish Guards in Prayer before Battle (Caton Woodville). '*Shortly before dawn on 15 September 1916, Fr Brown of the 1st Battalion came forward and collected half companies or groups of men as he could find them. Together they knelt on the shell churned ground, Protestant and Catholic, bare headed, their rifles with bayonets fixed by their sides while the small seemingly insignificant figure of the priest gave them Absolution. This simple scene seemed somehow to throw into relief the squalor and the filth, the glory and the sacrifice which was their war.*' (Kipling)

Below: **Ginchy Ridge** To the observer just another piece of undistinguished and indistinguishable landscape in a muddy, bloody world. But to those who took part a very special Hell. And that day the 'creepy-crawlies', the tanks, made their first, and inauspicious, appearance.

THE THIRD STAGE, 1916, The Somme

The Guards Division attacked with two brigades abreast each of four waves no more than fifty yards apart to take advantage of the massive artillery barrage, a guarantee of confusion should a leading wave be held up. To their right lay the Quadrilateral, a formidable German fortification. As was apt to happen, the attacking troops edged away from the point of most resistance thus the right-hand brigade found themselves advancing north rather than north-east and across the front of the other brigade. Soon the whole division had merged into an indescribable confusion of all lines and all regiments. But, as the chronicle records with feeling and not a little pride – 'The discipline held.'

An Irish Guards casualty at Ginchy is helped by Grenadier stretcher bearers during the assault on Ginchy Ridge, 15 September 1916.

SOMME 1916-18

Somme. Village of Ginchy, 1916.

Below: **Village of Ginchy, 1998.** German shells, ploughed up recently. The iron harvest.

Below: **Guards Division Memorial, Les Boeufs, near Ginchy.**

It was a time of heroics and great bravery, much of it unnoticed and unsung. Here Lt-Col J.V. Campbell of the Coldstream Guards won the Victoria Cross for rallying remnants of his own Battalion and a remarkable mix of strays of all sorts (with a silver hunting horn).

At Ginchy and in the ensuing fourteen days the two Battalions of Irish Guards lost over one thousand men.

Main road through Guillemont. After the Guards Division battle of 15 September 1916.

Back at Warley and the Guards Depot at Caterham, '*Yes, We made 'em – with the rheumatism on us and all; and we kept on making 'em till I got to hate the silly faces of 'em. And what did we get out of it? "Tell Warley that their last draft was damn rabbits and the Ensigns as bad." And after that, it's Military Crosses and* DCMs *for our damn rabbits.*' (Kipling)

Right: **Communication trench and grave,** west of Ginchy-Flers road. '*German shells bursting in our lines.*'

Leitrim Boy receives his Shamrock, St Patrick's Day 1917. Drum Major Fitzgerald looks on as Master Vickers places the Shamrock on Leitrim Boy's collar, which is held by Drummer Titman. The Pipers' (shown here are the 3rd Reserve Battalion, Warley) shoes have no buckles because when the first pipes were presented by John Redmond MP, the Master Shoemaker cut down the second pair of boots of the two pipers, and made the long tongues from the upper which he had removed. He could scrounge no suitable buckles, so to this day Irish Guards Pipers do not wear buckles. (Reminiscences of Sjt Gallacher, Royal Hospital)

CSM Toher receives the Military Medal for Bravery in the Field from Lord French who had succeeded Lord Kitchener as Colonel (at Warley on St Patrick's Day, 1917.) CSM Toher was the originator of the ever famous saying with reference to one of our own barrages: '*And even the wurrums themselves are getting up and crying for mercy.*'

THE FOURTH STAGE, 1917.

The Hindenburg Line, Passchendaele and Cambrai

Mainly as a result of the Somme Offensive, the Germans withdrew from the Somme to the Hindenburg Line in 1917, a distance of some 15 miles. This was more sudden than had been anticipated, and preparations were already in place for another offensive at Arras. The Guards Division was not involved, although it was in reserve for the attack on Messines Ridge. At this stage the French Armies were in serious difficulty and mutinies had broken out. To take the pressure off the French and allow them to restore the situation, the British mounted a further offensive at Ypres. This was the Third Battle of Ypres, otherwise known as Passchendaele. Its timing, recognised as critical because of the soil and the climate, was dictated by the urgent need to help the French, not as popular myth would suggest, by the stupidity of the General Staff.

Going up the line, Ypres, 1917 (Passchendaele). Silhouette of figures on skyline.

L/Sjt John Moyney VC. This self-effacing man found himself isolated with his section in no man's land during the 3rd Battle of Ypres (which he called 'Yepree'). With astonishing leadership and daring he held out, and eventually evacuated his section under heavy fire across the perilous Broembeek stream. He left the Regiment after the war, and was for many years the Station Master at Roscrea, Co. Tipperary. He marched on the St Patrick's Day Parade in 1982 at the Guards Depot, 'VC and all!'. He told an Irish newspaper interviewer that the VC had saved his life, for it had made him too famous to murder during the Troubles when ex-servicemen were hunted down in Ireland. (For full citation see p.206)

L/Cpl Thomas Woodcock VC, who lies among his regimental comrades. Thomas Woodcock was part of L/Sjt John Moyney's section, cut off in no man's land. He won his award in the withdrawal over the Broembeek by going back under fire, to try to rescue a comrade who had been with them through their ordeal and was killed in action in March 1918. This portrait must have been taken between October 1917, when his VC was Gazetted, and his death. (For full citation see p.207)

L/Cpl Woodcock's Grave at Achiet Le Petit cemetery.

Passchendaele, 1917.

Above: **Yser Canal after the attack involving 2nd Battalion,** 31 July 1917. The prodigious difficulties of the Third Battle of Ypres are amply illustrated in these photographs which show the dramatic difference between this battle and so-called conventional trench warfare.

While all this was happening a quiet young officer, Lt Hugh Lofting, was writing home to his young daughter. Allowing his imagination to wander away from the horrors, he composed imaginary conversations and fantasies. After the war these formed the basis for *Doctor Dolittle*, which he duly had published to world acclaim.

Lt-Col E.B. Greer MC, **July 1917, Commanding Officer of 2nd Battalion Irish Guards.** With Eric Greer's death the Regiment lost of one of its very finest officers. But the family connection continues. The photographer with the 1st Battalion Battle Group in Kosovo in 1999 was his grandson, Fergus Greer, who had served in the Regiment and who contributed many of the Balkan photographs

Air photograph of trench systems prior to the main attack and capture of Cambrai, 1918.

HAZEBROUCK

Lt Neville Marshall (seated behind trophy) with an Irish Guards football team. Acting Lt-Col Marshall MC* was posthumously awarded the Victoria Cross for his bravery when commanding a Battalion of the Lancashire Fusiliers in 1918. (For full citation see p. 207)

THE FIFTH STAGE, January–July 1918.
The German Offensive

The collapse of Russia in the revolution of 1917 closed Germany's Eastern Front, and thus enabled German strength on the Western Front to increase by one third. On the British side every brigade had effectively lost one of its four Battalions, sapped by the losses at Passchendaele, which had not been fully replaced. A new Fourth Guards Brigade was created (there having been but three brigades in the Guards Division), consisting of the 4th Grenadiers, 3rd Coldstream and 2nd Irish Guards. The Germans broke through, recapturing every yard of all the Somme gains, and more. An acute crisis developed as the Germans poured through in huge numbers dangerously close to the Channel Ports. There were no British reserves. 2nd Battalion Irish Guards fought in 4th Guards Brigade in an heroic last ditch effort near Hazebrouck (actually at a village called Vieux Berquin). In the process not only did 4th Guards Brigade cease to exist, but the component Battalions were so severely reduced during the engagement as to merge and blend into one ad hoc group, fighting as tenaciously as Guardsmen ever fought, backs to the wall. They held the German onrush and saved France. 2nd Battalion Irish Guards ceased thereafter to be operational, becoming, until the end of the war, a training Battalion for officers joining the Guards Division at Criel Plage.

Harry Robertshaw

7159 Pte Harry Robertshaw was killed with the 2nd Battalion Irish Guards near Ayette in the last stages of the German breakthrough on 28 March 1918. An Englishman in the Regiment, as had become more common as the war progressed, he had been wounded earlier in the war and evacuated to England. When he had regained his fitness he returned to the 2nd Battalion. The day he departed for the front he said to his sister: 'Please buy my friends a drink.' His sister remembered his words, and nearly seventy years later Mrs Lupton (Harry Robertshaw's sister) left a handsome bequest to the Regiment. Regimental Association dinners, St Patrick's Day drinks, and other special regimental occasions are subsidised by this generous bequest. Every time, a brief explanation of the story is given and the toast is drunk to the memory of Pte Harry Robertshaw. So when the Colours were trooped in 1996, the Irish Guards arranged that all the men on the Queen's Birthday Parade, regardless of regiment, would count as 'friends'. Each was given a specially labelled bottle of beer with lunch, showing the Irish Guards Colours, with the date, and stating that it was in memory of Pte Harry Robertshaw.

HINDENBURG LINE

Nearing the end. Advance over the canal at Maubeuge, not all that far from where they had first seen action over four years earlier.

The Canal du Nord (not a major battle honour of the Regiment, though one could be forgiven for wondering why not). This photograph gives an indication of the strength of the German defensive position. Here, after the capture, the Irish Guards cooks set up in one of the locks.

THE SIXTH STAGE, July–November 1918.
Advance to Victory: Canal du Nord, Hindenburg Line

ARMISTICE, 11am, 11 November 1918.
They began their last day, half an hour after midnight, marching 'as a Battalion' out of Bavai with their Lewis-gun limbers. Twice they were slightly shelled; once at least they had to unpack and negotiate more mine-craters at cross-roads. It was a populous world through which they tramped, and all silently but tensely awake – a world made up of a straight, hard road lumped above the level of the fields in places. Here and there one heard the chatter of a machine-gun, as detached and irrelevant as the laugh of an idiot. It would cease, and a single field-gun would open as on some private quarrel. Then silence, and a suspicion, born out of the darkness, that the road was mined. Next, orders to the Companies to spread themselves in different directions in the dark, to line ditches and the like for fear of attack. Thus dispersed, the Irish Guards received word that 'An Armistice was declared at 11a.m. this morning, November 11.'

Men took the news according to their natures. Indurated pessimists, after proving that it was a lie, said it would be but an interlude. Others retired into themselves as though they had been shot, or went stiffly off about the meticulous execution of some trumpery detail of kit-cleaning. Some turned round and fell asleep then and there; and a few lost all holds for a while. It was the appalling new silence of things that soothed and unsettled them in turn.
They did not realize till all sounds of their trade ceased,
and the stillness stung in their ears as soda-water stings on the palate, how entirely these had been part of their strained bodies and souls. ('It felt like falling through into nothing, ye'll understand. Listening for what wasn't there, and tryin' not to shout when you remembered for why.')

The two Battalions had lost in all two thousand three hundred and forty-nine dead, including one hundred and fifteen officers. Their total of wounded was five thousand seven hundred and thirty-nine.

They were too near and too deeply steeped in the War that year's end to realize their losses. Their early dead, as men talked over the past in Cologne, seemed to belong to immensely remote ages. Even those of that very spring, of whom friends could still say, 'If So-and-so had only lived to see this!' stood as far removed as the shadowy great ones of the pre-bomb, pre-duckboard twilight; and, in some inexpressible fashion, they themselves appeared to themselves the only living people in an uncaring world.

'But ye'll understand, when everything was said and done, there was nothing real to it at all, except when we got to talking and passing round the names of them we wished was with us.

'But ye might tell that we was lonely, most of all. Before God, we Micks was lonely!'

Kipling

Below left: **The irrepressible humour throughout the war,** as shown by this satirical cartoon in the Officers' Mess visitors' book used when out of the front line

---

Below: **The watch on the Rhine.**

Right: **Victory Medal.**

Far right: **Maubeuge,** 1918. Ptes Joseph and Brown, sentries on the Porte de Mons.

Announcing Armistice, Capts Barry and Paget 1st Battalion Irish Guards.

Marching towards Germany, halted in the Meuse Valley.

Irish Guards enter Cologne, 15 December 1918.

The Prince of Wales presents silk Union Flag (specifically not a Colour) to 2nd Battalion Irish Guards in Cologne, 14 January 1919. The filial was a spear head, not the royal crest normally borne on Colours.

Triumphal March through London. The world was in an unsettled state in 1919. For several reasons it was deemed sensible to let the capital know that the Guards were back. There was therefore held a magnificent triumphal march through London by the Guards Division. Two Irish Wolf Hounds attended.

Many discharged and wounded men were on parade, and the germ of the Regimental Association (first termed The Irish Guards Old Comrades Association) was undoubtedly sown. The King, mindful of the sacrifices and sterling work of the Foot Guards declared that henceforth Private Soldiers of the Foot Guards were officially to be termed Guardsmen. In addition, he decreed that the badge of rank worn by officers of the Foot Guards should cease to be the star of the Order of the Bath, and that each regiment should wear the star of the appropriate order of chivalry. Thereafter the Irish Guards officers have worn the star of the Order of St Patrick. Although the title Guardsman was not formally adopted until The King's decree after the war, the permanent headstones on graves of Private Soldiers of the Foot Guards of the Great War all carry the term Guardsmen. *L–R:* Lt D.A. Moodie, Sgt Lavery, Lt G. Tylden-Wright.

Post Script: Field Marshal Alex at the Dublin Reunion, 1960. The formalities over, he made immediately for two frail, elderly members with marvellous moustaches, 'I remember you at Bourlon Wood,' he said. They beamed. In an instant age fell from those old shoulders. To be replaced by ... Pride. Pride of association; Pride of achievement; Pride of 'Family' and Pride of Regiment.

In March 1938 the 1st Battalion moved to Mena Camp near the Pyramids.

CHAPTER THREE

1919–1938

BETWEEN THE WARS

One week after the Victory Parade in London, the 2nd Battalion was placed in suspended animation and their Union Flag, presented only eight weeks before in Cologne by the Prince of Wales, was laid up in the Roman Catholic Church at the Guards Depot, Caterham. No one on that emotional day would have guessed that only twenty years later the 2nd Battalion would have to be reactivated for another world war.

The spell of the 1st Battalion at home ended abruptly in May 1922, when they embarked to reinforce the Army of the Black Sea in Constantinople. Returning via Gibraltar they were back in England by April 1924.

Twelve years' home service followed until, in November 1936, the Battalion found itself in Egypt in Kasr el Nil Barracks, Cairo.

Their desert routine was rudely interrupted in July 1938, when they were suddenly ordered to Palestine to help keep order in a land even then of simmering discontent. Four hectic months on internal security duty ensued until, in November that year, they were ordered home.

By then war clouds were gathering and in anticipation of the conflict, in July 1939, the 2nd Battalion was reactivated. Shortly afterwards a Training Battalion was formed at Hobbs Barracks, Lingfield.

ST PATRICK'S DAY, 1919

Preparing for the parade. The 2nd Battalion wolfhound, Frank, and handler. Note the white lanyards worn on the left shoulder by the 2nd Battalion until 1919. Also just visible are the two green bars worn on the left sleeve indicating the 2nd Battalion.

Rudyard Kipling with officers and wives. His incomparable two volume *The Irish Guards in the Great War* was published in 1926 and was recently reprinted.

Tug of War. After men's dinners on St Patrick's Day it was traditional for a sports meeting to take place. Over the years this became a less formal affair.

The 2nd Battalion marching to church after the presentation of gallantry medals. The Regimental Serjeant Major and the Guardsman beside him are wearing DCMs, and the right hand man of the leading group wears both DCM and MM. There are six DCM winners and eleven MM winners to be seen leading the parade. No fewer than six members of the Regiment won a bar to their DCM, of whom most unusually two were Privates/ Guardsmen.

Final parade of the 2nd Battalion, 19 August 1919. Leaving Wellington Barracks, the wolfhound, Frank, leading.

The 1st and 2nd Battalion wolfhounds, Doran and Frank.

The King's Birthday Parade in Hyde Park, 3 June 1919. Number Seven Guard, Capt the Hon W.S. Alexander DSO; Lt G.L. St C. Bambridge MC; Lt E.C. FitzClarence. The parade was held in Hyde Park because Horse Guards Parade was still covered in wooden War Office huts.

Pipe Serpt Atkins.

Battalion cooks c.1920. Regimental cooks, under the leadership of the Master Cook, attracted many sobriquets. This individual, who is not in the photograph, was a member of the Battalion staff, addressed as 'Sir', and known by one and all as the 'Master Gyppo'.

Guardsmen Three –
Gdsm A. Duggan; L/Sjt J.
Moyney vc; Gdsm P. Dunn.

**Capt and Adjutant
J.S.N. FitzGerald** MBE,
MC. Known to all as
'Black Fitz', Colonel
Sidney served from
before the Great War and
was Regimental
Lieutenant Colonel for
most of the Second
World War.

**The 1st Battalion Irish Guards
Athletics Team**, 1921. Winners
of the inaugural Army Athletics
Championship. It was to be 44
years before the Regiment won
the championship again. It is not
often that the Commanding
Officer appears in athletics team
photographs as a competing
team member. In this case,
Lt-Col Harold Alexander, who
was a fine middle distance
runner, can be seen in his
athletics vest seated in front of
the man in white. That year he
won the Mile in the Army
competition.

At a moving ceremony at Windsor Castle the Colours of the old Irish Regiments were formally accepted into safe keeping by His Majesty King George V, 12 June 1922. (Royal Archives. By gracious permission of HM The Queen)

Magnificent silver inherited by the Irish Guards from the old Irish regiments.

The creation of the Irish Free State in 1922 meant the disbandment of the southern based Irish regiments. So passed into memory such redoubtable names as The Royal Irish Regiment (18th Foot), The Connaught Rangers (88th and 94th), The Leinster Regiment (Royal Canadians 100th and 104th), The Royal Munster Fusiliers (101st and 109th) and The Royal Dublin Fusiliers (102nd and 103rd). These infantry regiments bore reputations for courage and tenacity in the field second to none. The Colours were saved from the fire at Windsor Castle in November 1992, and are now on show in the restored State Apartments, thus fulfilling King George V's pledge to keep them safe.

Major. the Hon Harold. Alexander. D.S.O.

In May 1922 the 1st Battalion embarked for Turkey to reinforce the Army of the Black Sea endeavouring to keep peace between the Greeks and the Turks.

Preparing to entrain. A soldier's entire possessions travelled in his kitbag. They are seen here piled by companies.

The Corps of Drums marching at ease on their way to Windsor Station carrying slung rifles.

Right: **On arrival, the Drums and Fifes showed the flag at Pera.**

Far right: **The Commanding Officer receives his Shamrock** from the Commander-in-Chief, General Sir Charles Harrington, under whom they had served in the Great War.

Battalion Parade, Tash Kishla Barracks, Constantinople, 1923. On one such parade, the Battalion was entranced by the unexpected appearance of a delicious young lady, who rushed onto the square seeking her paramour of the night before: 'Eddy, Eddy,' she cried at full voice, 'Have you got my keys?'

TURKEY

A recurring dilemma has always been how to convey the Shamrock for St Patrick's Day to the far flung elements of the Regiment. Strange have been the methods adopted but they almost always succeed. In 1923 the situation was more acute for this was before the days of refrigeration. So it came about that three weeks before the great day, and courtesy of Imperial Airways, a withered and yellowed consignment duly arrived. It was shown to the Commanding Officer, Lt-Col the Hon. H.R. Alexander DSO, MC. Colonel Alex was horrified but the Quartermaster, Capt H. Hickie MBE, MC, rose to the occasion, 'Leave it to me, Sir. I will get it right for the day.'

But as St Patrick's Day loomed there was still no sign of the Shamrock and whenever the Commanding Officer raised the subject the Quartermaster was curiously evasive. At length Alex could bear it no longer. He must see it for himself. So together they wound their way down into the great cool cellars of the barracks to that holy-of-holies, the realms of the Quartermaster. Finally they came on the Shamrock and there it lay as green and as fresh as the day it had left Ireland. 'Hickie, you've achieved a miracle,' Alex exclaimed, 'what did you do?' 'Well, Sir,' came the reply, 'I just gave it some of what you and I like best. I gave it a sup of Irish whiskey.'

Officers of the 1st Battalion Irish Guards, Aldershot, 1926.
3rd Row: 2/Lt V.V. Gilbart-Denham; 2/Lt J.O.E. Vandeleur; 2/Lt Creehan, Rev J. McGuinness, Chaplain; 2/Lt Montagu-Douglas-Scott; Capt and Quartermaster H. Hickie MBE, MC; Lt R.C. Alexander
2nd Row: Capt T. Nugent; Lt T.A. Hacket-Pain; Lt E.R. Mahony; Lt T.H.H. Grayson; Lt F. Kellet; Lt T. Lindsay; Lt J. Repton; Capt D. Murphy
Seated: Capt Hon. W. Alexander DSO; Capt W.D. Faulkner MC; Colonel Hill-Child; Field Marshal The Earl of Cavan KP, Colonel of The Regiment; Lt-Col R.V. Pollok CBE, DSO, Commanding Officer; Capt R.B.S. Reford MC; Capt K.W. Hogg.

Irish Guards Old Comrades Association Dinner, 1927. The Old Comrades Association was formed after the Great War to enable friends to keep in touch with one another and to help members of the Regiment to find employment. The provision of welfare assistance soon began to be necessary, particularly for wounded old comrades. An annual dinner has been held by each branch ever since. The Association, now renamed the Irish Guards Association, continues to fulfil the same role.

Above: **Winners of the Connaught Cup for Infantry Chargers.** Twenty-one teams competed in Aldershot in 1929. The Regiment is nowadays not renowned for its prowess in the horse world with one or two notable exceptions. However, in this photograph the Commanding Officer, Second-in-Command, Adjutant and Company Commanders, all formally mounted officers, competed against the rest of the Army at home. Lt Jim Matthew; Major the Viscount (Hugo) Gough MC; Capt Bruce Reford MC; Lt Moose Alexander; Capt Francis (Pokey) Law MC; Capt Kenneth Hogg; Lt Edward Donner; Major Sidney FitzGerald MBE, MC; Capt Andy Pym, *Standing:* Lt-Col Val Pollok CBE, DSO.

The St Patrick's Day feast. In 1932 there was no central messing so this meal was held in barrack rooms. The Victorian Barracks in the Marlborough Lines at Aldershot did not have mess rooms at this time. Capt Tris Grayson with his Company.

King's Birthday Parade,
1932. Numbers 5 and 6
Guards found by the
Battalion.
5 Guard
Capt C.L.J. Bowen;
2/Lt the Hon B.A. O'Neill;
Lt H.C. McGildownay.
6 Guard
Major the Hon W.S.P.
Alexander DSO;
2/Lt D.H. FitzGerald;
Lt H.M. Taylor.

Many of those on Parade
were later to form the
backbone of the Battalion
in Norway in 1940.

St Patrick's Day Ball,
1933, Aldershot. The
etiquette of the time
required booking
partners for dances
during the evening.

Father McGuinness.

Lieut. J.B. Keenan.

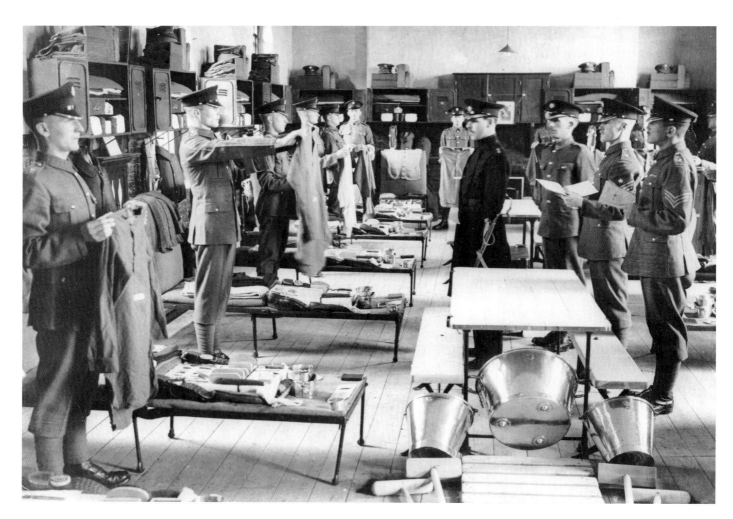

Kit Inspection, *c.*1930s. The Guards Depot, Caterham contained a company from each regiment of Foot Guards which was totally manned by staff from the regiment. No 5 Company Irish Guards had the role of converting raw recruits into Guardsmen, a task involving drill, fitness (PT), weapon training (rifle, bayonet, and 36 Grenade), discipline and meticulous attention to detail. Here a company officer carries out a formal kit inspection. Note the burnished tea buckets and the gleaming larger bucket (with small feet) in the centre.

Officers and Other Ranks still serving, who went to France with the 1st Battalion, 12 August 1914 – 12 August 1934. *Standing:* Gdsm (Pte) J. O'Connell; Gdsm (Pte) D. Foran; Gdsm (Pte) J. McInerney; Gdsm (Pte) P. Seagrave; Sjt P. Cronin. *Seated:* D/Sjt (L/Cpl) J. McGann; Lt QM (CQMS) P. Mathews; Lt-Col (Lt) J.S.N. FitzGerald MBE, MC; RSM (L/Cpl) J. Linnane MM; Sjt (Sgt) R. McCabe MM.

MASCOT DESERTS THE IRISH GUARDS

AND JOINS UP WITH THE COLDSTREAMERS

BY THE CULPRIT

I had a rare bit of fun to-day.

I am a wolf-hound, and, though I say it myself, as fine a wolf-hound as you'll find anywhere. The Irish Guards have adopted me as their mascot. I go on parade with them, and behave very solemnly. You know what parades are, and how fussy the Guards are about them.

To-day a drummer boy who often takes me out said, "Come along, Tiny" (I am so big that of *course* I have to be called Tiny), and took me in what I think you call the dickey seat of a motor-car.

Just as we got to Buckingham Palace I heard a band. The Changing of the Guard. I wanted to have a look, to see if the Coldstreamers are as smart as our fellows. (Our fellows always swear they're not.) But the car wouldn't stop.

So out I jumped, dragging the drummer boy with me.

I soon shook him off, and, dodging sentries and policemen, ran into the courtyard of the Palace and started to watch the Coldstreamers. The crowd at the Palace gates who had also come to watch the Coldstreamers stopped watching them to watch *ME*!

Just as I was getting interested in the "Old Guard, Present Hipe!" "New Guard, Present Hipe!" stuff I noticed the drummer boy and several policemen approaching.

I bolted.

* * *

Into the Green Park, round the Victoria Fountain, up The Mall I went. By this time lots of ordinary people were after me, and just as I was wondering what to do I saw a batch of Coldstreamers marching down The Mall and had an IDEA.

As they reached me I fell in with them and solemnly marched along at their head, just as though they were my own mob.

I was enjoying the situation thoroughly when that pesky little drummer boy stole up at my back, grabbed my collar, and yanked me back to barracks. Bad cess to him!

Still, I'd had my fun.

* * *

REFLECTION: Lucky for me I'm a mascot, not an "other rank." What a charge-sheet there'd be to face in the morning—"Absent from parade," "Unsoldierly conduct," and goodness only knows what.

Here I am, bolting through the gates of the Palace.

Cruachan goes absent! Evidently a considerable character, he unfortunately developed a strong dislike for the Italian Ambassador's poodle and, after savaging it one day in Hyde Park, some weeks later he went further and killed it. So followed his premature retirement. No replacement was sought until 1942.

The King's Birthday Parade, 1935. The last attended by King George V. His Majesty, seen here wearing the star of the Order of St Patrick, accompanied by the Regimental Lieutenant Colonel, J.S.N. FitzGerald MBE, MC. (Royal Archives. By gracious permission of HM The Queen).

Farewell to the Horse, August 1936. The Transport Platoon became the Mechanical Transport Platoon. The change took place at Pirbright (the old black huts are visible in the background). The Transport Platoon under Lt A.S. Lockwood comprised one General Service Wagon (centre), the Battalion cooker (right), incorporating a Sawyer stove introduced after the Crimean War, and the ammunition limber (left). The Field Officers' chargers are in the front. The platoon commander, as a mounted officer, wore boots and breeches.

Welcome to the First Mechanical Transport Platoon. The platoon grew to 38 strong and contained four 15cwt trucks known as Bugs, as well as two dispatch riders ('Don Rs') and three Austin Seven convertible cars with civilian registration numbers. No longer a mounted officer, the platoon commander reverted to puttees.

One day in 1936, with the Adjutant on leave and a soporific air settled over the Battalion, the acting adjutant, nosing under the blotter on his desk, came on a highly disturbing letter. To everyone's horror it revealed that in thirty-six hours The King himself was coming to witness a first demonstration of the change from drilling in fours to drilling in threes. No one knew of this, no one had tried it out, no one had practised it. The result, however, was deemed highly satisfactory!

CoL.
R.C.A.
McCalmont.
D.S.O.

Postscript: Seizing on the moment in a rehearsal for The 1939 King's Birthday Parade, when the guards unwind after a form, the German press made much of the fact that the Irish Guards appeared unable to keep their dressing. To refute this monstrous accusation and show that in fact the Micks could and indeed were wont to march in straight lines, the *Daily Mail* unearthed the previous picture.

EGYPT

In November 1936 the Battalion embarked for Egypt. They were stationed at Kasr el Nil Barracks, Cairo.

Training in the desert had its peculiarities.

Below: **Semaphore.** Semaphore, favoured by the Royal Navy, was a much practised art. In this picture of training in Egypt a Signal Platoon semaphore team of Sender, Reader, Runner and NCO in charge can be seen.

Above: **The Signal Platoon in training near the Pyramids using heliographs.** This method of using Morse code by flashes of sunlight from a mirror was exceptionally effective and allowed brief messages to be sent prodigious distances in a very short time. Regiments of the Indian Army wore polished flat waist belt clasps, pierced with holes (which normally accommodated a regimental brass insignia), which when taken off could be used as heliographs. Old soldiers may remember the small metal shaving mirrors issued with a hole in the centre which were designed for the same purpose.

The Intelligence Platoon under Capt J.O.E. Vandeleur who had previously commanded a camel company in the Sudan. On his left, Drummer Thackrah who was later awarded a Military Medal in Palestine, and went on to become a Regimental Serjeant Major in The Gloucestershire Regiment during the Second World War.

PALESTINE

The desert routine was interrupted in July 1938 when they were suddenly ordered to Palestine where an uprising was simmering. Four months of intensive internal security operations followed.

Principal transport were the commandeered donkey lorries seen here full to overflowing with the Instant Response Platoon.

The wireless lorry was the only communication with base.

The ubiquitous donkey was the universal carrier. The Battalion was allocated thirty of these beasts and had 'found' an extra one during an operation in the hills – 'the strongest and most obstinate donkeys in all Palestine', they declared. When normal urging was unsuccessful they resorted to lighting dried grass under their bellies. The effect was electric! The sun helmets carried a bronzed and enlarged cap star.

Patrolling. The last man carries a grenade launcher on his rifle. The uniform looks to the modern eye to be unsuitable for patrolling in rough, hot, prickly country. Full 1908 pattern web equipment wearing Khaki Drill with shorts, boots, puttees and hose tops (with blue-red-blue tops) and sun helmets!

Cars were meticulously searched at checkpoints manned by the Battalion . . .

. . . sometimes yielding a rich haul, in this case of ancient firearms, bandoliers and landmines.

Ambush. At this point in the track near the town of Saffit an Irish Guards Platoon truck with a Lewis Gun and a Rolls Royce armoured car of the 11th Hussars ran into an ambush. The leading truck was blown up by a mine and one man was killed and five wounded. The SOS platoon was called up, and with air support from the RAF, 15 rebels were accounted for.

One fighter was shot down, the pilot and observer both killed. To destroy the aircraft, its bomb and armaments and prevent them falling into the rebels' hands, Capt Michael Gordon-Watson ran down under heavy sniper fire and set fire to the machine. He was awarded the first of his three Military Crosses.

In November 1938 the Battalion returned to England.

Guardsmen returning from training at Pirbright in 1938. Here the newly issued 1938 Pattern blancoed web equipment has replaced the 1908 pattern. The helmets are still painted a pale (Palestine) colour, and bagged bearskins are part of the standard equipment when the Battalion is in London District. (Pirbright was part of London District until the 1990s.)

On return from Palestine the Battalion was stationed in the Tower of London, just as it had been shortly before the Great War. Here Capt Basil Eugster (later General Sir Basil Eugster KCB, KCVO, CBE, DSO, MC, Colonel of the Regiment 1969–1984) leaves Waterloo Station (wearing his newly won first Military Cross ribbon) at the head of No 1 Company as they march to the Tower of London.

General Service Medal. Clasp Palestine.

Military Medals being presented at the Tower of London by the Major-General, A.F.A.C. Thorne CMG, DSO. *L–R:* Sjt. T. Millar; L/Cpl J. Thackrah; L/Cpl D. Murphy; L/Cpl W. Rooney and the Major-General having been received with a General Salute is addressing the parade. The Commanding Officer, in a frock coat, has his sword drawn (not easy to return when the scabbard is unslung).

In the Foot Guards it was customary to spell Serjeant with a 'j' until 1939. However, the rest of the Army preferred to use a letter 'g'. In an urge to modernise and standardise the Foot Guards reluctantly decided to conform in 1952.

Field Marshal The Earl of Cavan KP, GCB, GCMG, GCVO, GBE.

With the crisis in Europe deepening, war clouds gathered once again. In expectation of conflict the 2nd Battalion was reformed.

The cemetery at Medjez-el-Bab.

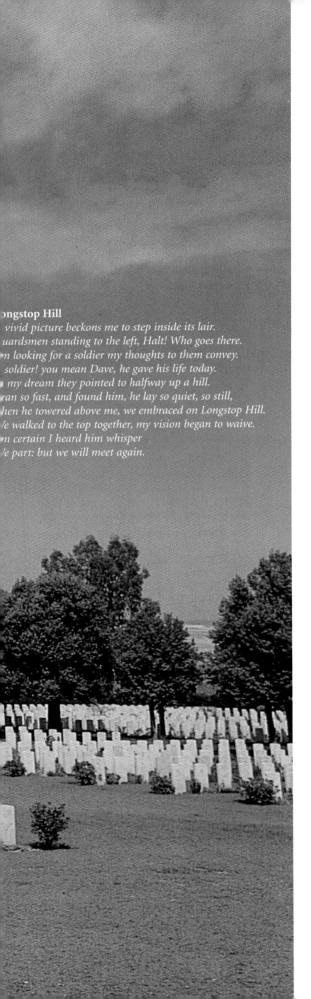

...ongstop Hill

*...vivid picture beckons me to step inside its lair.
...uardsmen standing to the left, Halt! Who goes there.
...n looking for a soldier my thoughts to them convey.
...soldier! you mean Dave, he gave his life today.
...my dream they pointed to halfway up a hill.
...ran so fast, and found him, he lay so quiet, so still,
...hen he towered above me, we embraced on Longstop Hill.
...e walked to the top together, my vision began to waive.
...n certain I heard him whisper
...e part: but we will meet again.*

CHAPTER FOUR

1939–1945

THE SECOND WORLD WAR

When war was declared on 3 September 1939, both Battalions were at Wellington Barracks. Rumours were rife as to where the Irish Guards might be first committed. It turned out to be Norway where the 1st Battalion was to suffer a devastating first blow.

While the 1st Battalion was so engaged, the 2nd Battalion found themselves acting as covering force for the evacuation of the Dutch Royal family from the Hook of Holland. Ten days later they were helping with the evacuation of the BEF from Boulogne.

As part of the the build up to the eventual invasion of Europe, it was decided to create the Guards Armoured Division. So in the autumn of 1941 the 2nd Battalion converted to tanks.

While the 2nd (Armoured) and newly created 3rd Battalions trained in England, the 1st Battalion once more embarked for foreign shores on 1 March 1943. This time to North Africa, where the Regiment earned immortal fame at the Battle of the Bou.

The invasion of Sicily and later mainland Italy left the 1st Battalion unaffected until the amphibious landing at Anzio thirty miles south of Rome in January 1944. Here, in a short campaign of unexampled ferocity, while adding new laurels to the Regiment's name, the 1st Battalion effectively ceased to exist.

On D+17, the Guards Armoured Division landed in Normandy, and from then until the end of the war eleven months later, the 2nd and 3rd Battalions saw almost unceasing action in France, Belgium, Holland and finally Germany itself. Early in the conflict it was decided to create regimental groups each consisting of an armoured and infantry Battalion. So it was as the Irish Guards Group that the Regiment latterly fought in Northwest Europe.

Presentation of Colours to the 2nd Battalion by His Majesty King George VI, Wellington Barracks, London, 16 February 1940. Major T. G. Lindsay; 2/Lt G.G. Romer; Lt J.D. Hornung; Major E.R. Mahoney. An unusual order of dress was the wearing of a blue-grey greatcoat over Service Dress with field boots and breeches which took the place of home service clothing in war time. This photograph was taken during the 'Phoney War' when the British Expeditionary Force was in France, and the Germans had not yet invaded France, Belgium or Holland. In the next few weeks both Battalions of the Regiment earned major battle honours in Norway (1st Battalion) and at Boulogne (2nd Battalion).

Mounting King's Guard at Buckingham Palace. The 1st Battalion wear steel helmets and carry respirators. Memories of gas in the Great War, and speculation on German capability to deliver gas attacks from the air brought about the insistence that civilians as well as the armed services carry respirators at all times. Since the respirator was worn slung over the left shoulder and crossed the Sam Browne belt's cross strap, the strap was temporarily taken out of use.

The Regimental Band in Hackney, 1940. The Regimental Band wore the old pattern Service Dress and Service Dress caps.

1939–45 Star, awarded for six months'* service in an operational command, except for service in Dunkirk, Norway, some specified commando raids, and other services for which the qualifying service was one day. The ribbon, as with the whole series of Second World War campaign stars, was selected by The King. The 1939–45 Star (originally known as the 1939–40 Star) represents the colours of the three armed services in equal proportions.

*For the purposes of the Army, a month has thirty days when it comes to decorations!

NORWAY

Both the Battalions were in Wellington Barracks, London when on 10 April 1940, to the chagrin of their sister Battalion, the 1st Battalion went to Norway. Speculation had been rife as to which Battalion would go to war first, and where it would go.

Left: **Seeing off the Battalion**. The Adjutant, Capt the Hon B.A. O'Neill; Commanding Officer, Lt-Col W.D. Faulkner MC and the Second-in-Command Major C.L.J. Bowen. On the evening of that day the Battalion paraded on the square in their new battledress and piled aboard Green Line buses scrawled with such messages as 'To Norway', 'See the Midnight Sun', 'The North Pole Express'. So Norway it was to be. To the well-used valediction 'Keep your head down, Mick' from their comrades, the 1st Battalion were piped away from barracks. This was the first public airing of the new battledress.

The ubiquitous 'puffers', the local fishing boats, were used to ferry the companies ashore.

Capt F.R.A. Lewin, later killed in the *Chobry*, and 2/Lt G.P.M. FitzGerald in Arctic order.

NORWAY 1940

THE *CHOBRY*

On 13 May 1940, the same day that the Germans invaded the Low Countries, the Battalion sailed south from Narvik on board the former Polish liner, *Chobry*, to reinforce the flimsy line attempting to hold the inexorable German advance up through Norway. It was the time of perpetual daylight in those latitudes and at midnight they were attacked by a force of Heinkel bombers. Striking amidships, all the bombs exploded near the senior officers' cabins, killing the Commanding Officer, the Second-in-Command and the Adjutant. Of the five company commanders, Major T.A. Hacket-Pain and Capt J.R. Durham-Matthews were killed outright. Major V.V. Gilbart-Denham died later, while both the other company commanders were wounded. Three Guardsmen were also killed in the attack.

A blazing inferno now divided the ship and the Regimental Sergeant-Major, Johnnie Stack, formed up the Battalion on the foredeck awaiting rescue. The one officer present was the Battalion priest, Father 'Pop' Cavanagh, and so, on a burning ship in the Arctic, bare-headed, the Guardsmen said the prayers they had learned in the quiet churches and farmsteads of Ireland, as their forebears had once done on the battlefields of France.

With great gallantry, and expecting *Chobry* to blow up at any moment, the attendant destroyer HMS *Wolverine* pulled alongside. Using gangways and ropes the Battalion filed aboard. Command devolved on the senior surviving fit officer, Capt D.M.L. Gordon-Watson MC.

'I never before realised what the discipline of the Guards was ... There was no confusion, no hurry, and no sign of haste or flurry ... Their conduct in the most trying circumstances, in the absence of senior officers, on a burning ship, open at any time to a new attack, was as fine, or finer than, the conduct in the old days of the soldiers on the Birkenhead. It may interest you to know that 694 men were got on board in sixteen minutes.'

Extract from a letter from the late Commander Craske, RN, Captain of HMS *Wolverine*.

Father 'Pop' Cavanagh.

RSM Stack who was awarded the Military Cross for his outstanding leadership that day. The sole warrant officer in the Regiment to be awarded the Military Cross in World War Two.

Chobry after the German attack. The Captain of *Chobry*, a gallant Pole, asked Commander Craske of HMS *Wolverine* to take a photograph of *Chobry* lest he be falsely accused of abandoning his ship unnecessarily. It can be seen that the bow and the stern of the ship are separated by the inferno amidships.

HOOK OF HOLLAND

On 12 May 1940, the day before the 1st Battalion sailed south from Narvik in *Chobry*, the 2nd Battalion embarked hurriedly at Dover bound for some unknown destination. This turned out to be the small port of Hook of Holland and it transpired they were there to cover the evacuation of the Dutch Royal Family and the Dutch government in face of the advancing German army. Two days later they returned to Dover.

The dockside at Boulogne as the Battalion deploys in support of the BEF.

Closing moments. HMS *Wild Swan* sent a large German tank on the opposite quay spinning like a cartwheel, and blasted the top floor off an hotel when she spotted a machine-gun firing on the Battalion from an upper window. Father Julian Stonor wrote: '*It was dark when I came on deck from the inferno below. I found a seat on a torpedo tube with some Guardsmen and we talked about the sea and our admiration for these sailors.*'

BOULOGNE

Eight days later, in company with the 2nd Battalion Welsh Guards, they were off again, this time to Boulogne to try to buy time for the BEF's evacuation from Calais and Dunkirk.

The Germans were closing fast and the perimeter shrinking ominously. In this situation of imminent danger the Battalion priest, Father Julian Stonor, embarked on his personal crusade. Running from slit trench to slit trench he gave everyone Absolution. As he later wrote, '*any number, and not all of them Catholics, told me afterwards that from that moment onwards they felt no fear*'.

Pressed from all sides and under fire from Germans now crowding the hills overlooking the harbour, the remains of the two Battalions re-embarked. Each left behind nearly 200 Officers and Other Ranks killed, wounded or missing.

Above left: **Father Julian Stonor** who recorded '*With such a deafening noise of machine-guns I never thought I would be able to do more than one or two trenches, but as each trench directed me to the next and still nothing hit me, I, too, lost all sense of fear; all the more exposed a man was, the more exhilaration I got out of going to see him.*'

Above right: **Lt-Col Charles Haydon** DSO, OBE, **Commanding Officer, 2nd Battalion Irish Guards.** He was awarded the DSO for Hook of Holland and Boulogne, and earned another later as a brigadier.

The Bridge Emblem of HMS *Whitshed* which carried the 2nd Battalion at both Hook of Holland and Boulogne. Her close support during the evacuation from the port was crucial.

His Majesty The King, dressed as Colonel-in-Chief, visited the 1st Battalion in July 1940 at Northwood, Middlesex, on their return from Norway.

The King awarded DCMs to L/Cpl J. Wylie; Gdsm T. Callaghan; Gdsm M. O'Shea and Sgt W. Johnstone; Also a bar to his Military Cross to Capt D.M.L. Gordon-Watson MC. The Distinguished Conduct Medal was introduced in 1854 (i.e. before the Victoria Cross) for 'NCOs and Privates only'. It ranked next below the VC in soldiers' gallantry awards. It was discontinued in 1994. Sgt Johnno Johnstone, Medical Sergeant on the *Chobry*, became a revered Quartermaster in the 1960s. Gdsm O'Shea was orderly to Michael Gordon-Watson throughout the war, a highly hazardous occupation!

Wartime use of the Northwood Golf Course.

The Distintinguished Conduct Medal.

BUILD UP

Shortly after the Battalion returned from Norway, Lt-Col Edmund Mahony, from Galway, took over command at Northwood. Touring barracks one morning with the Adjutant, Capt Basil Eugster, MC, they were surprised to see a staff car draw up. A self-important, red-tabbed sub area commander emerged. *'Who is this man; are we expecting him?'* asked Colonel Edmund of the Adjutant, *'Show him the latrines!'* and stalked off. One did not call on the Irish Guards uninvited.

Bayonet Practice. *L–R:* Capt Michael Gordon-Watson with blackthorn walking stick, The King, Colonel Edmund Mahony.

Purposeful PT wearing steel helmets decorated with a stylised regimental blue plume on the right.

St Patrick's Day, 1941, Hobbs Barracks, Lingfield. Lt (QM) A. Ashton; Lt-Col the Viscount Gough MC; Commanding Officer; Lt J.D. Moore, Adjutant; General Sir Alexander Godley GCB, KCMG (who had trained the Regiment's Mounted Infantry for the Boer War); Lt Col M. Marchant ATS; Major J.O.E. Vandeleur; Capt A.R. Pym; Capt D.J.B. FitzGerald; Capt G.A.M. Vandeleur; CSM Twomey; CSM McKenna; CSM White; 2/Lt M. Evans ATS.

Admirers!

Presiding over the Training Battalion in his own inimitable way was Lt-Col the Viscount Gough, who was the first officer to be decorated in the Regiment in the Great War, who lost an arm and won the Regiment's first Military Cross. Those who came under his influence remember their time with deep and abiding affection.

One day a Guardsman was brought before his Commanding Officer on a charge of being drunk and disorderly. He was no stranger to this court of justice, this giant of a man from County Clare, who later proved to be a fine fighting Mick.

In a weary tone Lord Gough enquired, '*So just how drunk were you this time, O'Donovan?*'

Came the winning reply: '*I thank you for leave to speak, my Lord; I was as drunk as a lord, my Lord.*'

The case was dismissed.

Lt-Col the Viscount Gough MC.

TRAINING BATTALION

The Training Battalion had been formed in April 1939 to handle the immense number of recruits now pouring in. Shortly after, they moved to Hobbs Barracks, Lingfield in Surrey which was to be their home until near the end of the war, with a brief interlude in July 1940 on anti-invasion duties at Dover.

At Lingfield the reinforcements for all three service Battalions were 'taught to become', above all, Guardsmen and Irish Guardsmen before being passed to holding units in the various theatres of operation. Not all remained as Irish Guardsmen, however. Others, including such luminaries as Spike Milligan, were given their basic training and then moved on to other regiments.

The Commanding Officer's tank was christened 'St Patrick', seen here with Sergeant Bob Gorton, its driver until the end of the war. The Adjutant's was 'St Columb'; Second-in-Command's 'Ulster'. The three squadron commanders, 'Munster', 'Leinster' and 'Connaught'. Within the squadrons, Number 1 had names beginning with 'A'; Number 2, 'B'; Number 3, 'C'. Troop Commanders in Number 1 Squadron used the prefix 'Ard. . .'; Number 2, 'Bally. . .'; Number 3, 'Castle. . .'. It was a simple, easily understood system which allowed for no confusion and it served the Battalion well.

SECOND BATTALION

In the autumn of 1941 the 2nd Battalion, then stationed at Woking, converted to tanks as part of the newly created Guards Armoured Division.

The doubters, of which there were a few, declared that Guardsmen could not physically fit inside tanks nor ever adapt to the swiftly moving panorama of armoured warfare. They were proved generally wrong on the first count and triumphantly wrong on the second.

The first tanks were Covenanters Mark I, very second-hand, flogged near to death, but the pride of the whole Battalion. Their first inspection was an armoured review in front of the Major-General. The four tanks behaved impeccably and only a few ill-humoured spectators remarked that they had seen rusty water coming from one of the barrels when dipped in salute!

Below left: **The carriers of the Carrier Troop** for forward resupply and casualty evacuation were named after places in Ireland beginning with the letter 'C' – here 'City of Cork'.

Below: **The dingo scout cars** of the Recce Troop used the letter 'D'.

The tanks continued to arrive, all second-hand at first, then one day a brand new one appeared and with that the Battalion reckoned their existence had been properly acknowledged.

The Covenanter weighed 18 tons, with a top speed of 31mph, but armed with a pea-shooter of a gun, a puny 2-pounder. Later Marks had a 6-pounder but experience in North Africa had already shown this too was no match for German armour.

There was a brief interlude with Crusaders, sleek, low-silhouetted, very fast with a wonderful suspension but still armed with the 6-pounder. Then one day, after returning from an exercise at Thetford in Norfolk, they found to greet them sixty gleaming new American Sherman tanks.

Much higher, with a crew of five rather than the three of Covenanter and Crusader, the Sherman was a different prospect altogether. Moreover, it was armed with a very fine 75mm gun. The Sherman, despite its tendency to brew up when hit, served the Battalion well, being able to deal with any enemy armour until in due time they came up against the monster German tank, the King Tiger.

The Colonel of the Regiment, Field Marshal The Earl of Cavan KP, GCB, GCMG, GCVO, GBE, takes the salute from a Crusader of the 2nd Battalion.

The Queen with Lt-Col Gerald Verney MVO, Commanding Officer 2nd Battalion Irish Guards. The censor has obliterated the divisional signs from the sleeves of battle dress and the tactical signs have been removed from the tanks to prevent identification. When the Guards Armoured Division went to Normandy, 2nd Armoured Battalion Irish Guards formed part of 5 Guards Armoured Brigade. Its tactical sign was the Ever Open Eye and the white number 53 on a red background.

2nd (Armoured) Battalion Irish Guards Battalion Headquarters, Spring 1942. This Battalion wore black berets, of which they were very proud.

Tommy Gun Practice at Fonthill. Lt Mick O'Cock receives instruction from Capt Terence O'Neill (later Prime Minister of Northern Ireland, Lord O'Neill of the Maine).

From L–R Front Row (seated):
RSM Robin Hastings; Lt Ronnie Robertson; Capt Will Berridge (Adjutant); Lt-Col Gerald Verney MVO; Capt George Denneby; Lt Patrick Pollock; Sgt Cross.

Second Row: L/Cpl Bricky Cardwell; Gdsm Laverick; L/Cpl Doran; Sgt Bob Gorton; Gdsm Lawless (transferred to Parachute Regiment); Gdsm Jock O'Neill, Gdsm McGuinness; Gdsm Spatcher.

Third Row:
Gdsm Ernie Lloyd (Despatch Rider); Gdsm Jack Bettam (Despatch Rider); Gdsm Hughie Williamson; Unidentified; Sgt Matt Fitzsimmons; Gdsm Yates; Gdsm Thackham; Gdsm George Knight (Driver of 'Erin').

Back Row:
Gdsm Ken Shaw; Sgt Chamberlain; Gdsm Victor Crampton.

Forming up on the drive of Fonthill House. The road to the training areas on Salisbury Plain passed through the charming village of Wylye. Wylye's Days of Horror, as the ensuing period was known, became memorable to the long-suffering inhabitants who stoically endured the vagaries of Mick tanks. Many of the drivers had never driven anything in their lives, and the steering of the Covenanters was notoriously unreliable and prone inexplicably to fail altogether. Hence, as the Regimental history cheerfully records, hardly a day passed without the Battalion leaving its mark.

On one occasion a tank slewed uncontrollably off the road ending up in the front room of a house where two old ladies had been quietly having tea. When asked to remove his offending monster the tank commander was forced to point out that were he to do so the house would assuredly fall down. Whereupon the imperturbable pair invited him and his crew to join them for tea!

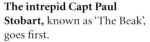

Building a footbridge under the watchful eye of Lt Oliver Chesterton and to the huge amusement of everyone else.

Capt Morrogh O'Brien.

The intrepid Capt Paul Stobart, known as 'The Beak', goes first.

HOME DEFENCE

Purposeful home defence exercises formed an integral part of training in England. With a fine sense of the ridiculous, one such exercise was held at Woking in which the 2nd Battalion was required to flush out pretend German parachutists and Fifth Columnists (spies). It will be noted that in the photograph showing the prisoner under escort the Guardsmen are wearing respirator cases and side caps.

Skulking.

Rumbled.

Under escort, Major Jack Thursby.

Interrogation about to commence.

The Defence Medal was awarded for service in non-operational areas subjected to air attack or closely threatened, provided such service lasted for three or more years. Its ribbon, flame coloured with green edges, is symbolic of enemy attacks on 'our green and pleasant land'. The two black stripes represent the black-out.

NORTH AFRICA

On 1 March 1943 the 1st Battalion embarked at Liverpool on board the P&O liner *Strathmore*. Their destination was North Africa as reinforcement to 1st Army which had landed the previous November. In conjunction with the 8th Army, operating from the south, it was conducting a massive pincer movement designed to squeeze the Germans out of North Africa and Tunisia in particular.

Preliminary operations involved patrolling, followed by a gallant night attack by No 2 Company on Recce Ridge. The company, lacking proper intelligence, set off quietly across the plain at dusk to attack the feature. The Battalion heard wild firing in the distance, and then nothing. Several weeks later it took a full divisional attack to capture Recce Ridge. Only a handful of Irish Guardsmen, mostly wounded, had survived and they were taken prisoner. The full story of Recce Ridge was not known until after the war when the prisoners came home. At the time of writing (1999) two survivors are still alive. The minor battle honour, not carried on the Colours, *Medjez Plain*, was awarded for the operations.

The key to the town of Tunis, and ultimately to Tunisia itself, was the narrow neck of the Medjez Valley some thirty miles west of the town. At its eastern end the valley is some four miles across but dominated by a major feature, Djebel Bou Aoukaz, the 'Bou'.

Towards the end of 21 April, Guards Brigade, comprising 1st Irish Guards, 1st Scots Guards and 5th Grenadiers, were committed to clearing the corridor. On 27 April the Irish Guards were ordered to capture two important features, Points 212 and 214.

The attack was straight up a plain dominated to the left by a well established enemy. It had originally been planned for the night of the 27th, but at noon this was brought forward to four o'clock in broad daylight in the heat of the afternoon.

The Africa Star was awarded to 1st Battalion Irish Guards with the clasp First Army, with a silver figure 'I' worn when only the ribbon is worn.

Memorial Cross erected on Point 212 to commemorate those Irish Guardsmen who gave their lives taking and defending the Bou.

Sgt Desmond Lynch
DCM. Awarded his DCM at the Battle of the Bou, Desmond Lynch was RSM at the Indian Military Academy and then at both Eaton Hall and Mons Officer Cadet Schools under the then Brigadier Basil Eugster. His last appointment after retirement was Assistant Adjutant RMA Sandhurst.

JEBEL BOU AOUKAZ, 27 April 1943

Point 214

Point 212

With their approach dominated by the high ground to their left, the Battalion suffered appalling casualties in the cornfields and well-defended olive groves in the open ground. *'They threw everything but their cap-badges at us. Guns, mortar, and those abominable machines the six-barrel mortars, everything within miles let drive. The platoons spread out into open order and plunged into the waist-high corn. The fire intensified and the whole cornfield was ripped and torn. Part of it was burning smokily. Amid the tall poppies that stood out over the corn there sprang a new crop – rifle butts. They appeared so suddenly, and so quickly, that it was almost a surprise to look beyond them and see the thin line of men plodding steadily on towards the olive grove. "We could not believe it," said a German prisoner afterwards. "We thought no one could cross that plain." A Guardsman put it more succinctly. "Thank God for drill, it keeps you going." (FitzGerald)'* In 1949 D.J.L FitzGerald MC, Adjutant of the 1st Battalion 1943–44, wrote *A History of The Irish Guards in the Second World War*, generally acknowledged as one of the finest military histories of that war. In it he wrote:

At dusk 173 men, all that had survived from four full rifle companies, and forward elements of Battalion Headquarters, struggled up the slopes of Points 212 and 214 beyond, and were promptly cut off by Germans swarming in behind them. Three days later 80 men, which included a smattering of reinforcements who had been able to get through the German cordon to the little beleaguered force, were finally relieved having resisted incessant and persistent attacks to uproot them.

In 1987 a regimental tour visited the Bou. Major Sir Oliver Chesterton MC, standing on the top of what had

South

1st Irish Guards approach

187 GAB GAB GAP

DJEBEL BOU AOUKAZ 1943

Looking down from Point 212 to the Olive Groves and startline.

After the battle. Father Dolly Brookes said Mass with the survivors on Point 212 after the dedication of the Memorial Cross. Father Dolly, Adjutant of the 2nd Battalion in the Great War, priest and friend to all thereafter, had persuaded three Germans, by use of his blackthorn stick, to help him look for the wounded in the cornfield. 'There are not words strong enough to express the shining example Father Brookes gave to all ranks ... he has been in places where the fire was impossibly heavy, and yet has given comfort to the dying without any thought for his safety ... an almost unbelievable devotion to duty and bravery ... never appearing too tired to go to the furthest points to help a wounded man ... the admiration of all. The sight of Father Brookes pacing up and down reading his breviary under heavy fire has restored the confidence of many a shaken man' (extract from citation for the Military Cross).

been called 'Oliver's Hill' because he was the first officer to reach the top, said that he had a guilty conscience about the Bou. He had been wounded twice in the cornfield. *'Ducking and weaving like a Welsh fly half, I was.'* He was carrying a Tommy gun and a grenade. He pulled the pin from the grenade with his teeth, like a film star, and fought his way to the summit. Then, seeing two Germans in a shell scrape, he chucked it at them. *'And I've always felt guilty about that. We'd lost so many men, and we were angry, but they weren't actually harming anyone then.'* From among the veterans present on the tour came a voice: *'Don't worry any more, Sir. That grenade never went off. You hadn't cleaned it!'* It was Gdsm Crawford, his orderly from 1943, who had travelled from Australia to be there.

Lt-Col Andrew Montagu-Douglas-Scott was awarded an immediate DSO as was Capt Colin Kennard who had so dominated the defence of Point 214. Also given were two Military Crosses, four DCMs and seven Military Medals after an epic which was to go down as one of the great stands in the Second World War.

Then in August they heard that L/Cpl John Kenneally (now L/Sgt) had been awarded the Victoria Cross. (For full citation see p. 209.)

Marching to the Victory Service in Carthage Cathedral, May 1943. As the noise of the pipes was heard one of the white-robed priests sprang from his stall and rushed down the aisle crying. 'I must see the boys, I must.' His name in religion was Pere Angelicus but he had been born Flynn and came from County Westmeath.

On 27 August General Alexander made the presentation. The Battalion was formed up on three sides of a square and, after carrying out a full inspection, L/Sgt Kenneally was marched out to receive his ribbon. Then with Kenneally standing on the saluting base to his right, the Battalion marched past. RSM McLaughlin and L/Sgt Kenneally VC.

ANZIO

In July 1943 the invasion of Sicily commenced. On 9 September took place the first landing on 'Fortress Europe' at Salerno. Then winter clamped down on Italy and stalemate ensued. To break the stalemate, to by-pass the opposition and make use of the available landing craft before they left the Mediterranean bound for home, OPERATION OVERLORD and D-Day, an amphibious operation was mounted thirty miles south of Rome at the seaside resort of Anzio. To veterans of that campaign in the Italian spring of 1944 the name recalls memories of death in appalling conditions of mud and cold, and of a battle so nearly lost. The Germans described it as the Allies' 'Epic of Bravery'.

The hell hole of Anzio and the notorious Wadis. Here in a world of savagery their skill at arms, pride of Regiment and sheer bloody-mindedness brought them through.

A scene of peace! The first morning, General Alex, Supreme Allied Commander, and the Naval C-in-C, Admiral Troubridge, on the beach as a member of the pioneer platoon sweeps the ground they are standing on for mines!

L/Cpl Doak with two German prisoners

The Road to Rome. View of the Via Anziate taken five days after the landing. An inviting prospect and only thirty miles from Rome but overlooked from the Alban Hills behind, with a water-table only just below the surface and opposed by a resourceful foe – recipe for a bitter war.

ANZIO

On 27 February the remnants of 1st Battalion Irish Guards were withdrawn from Anzio, a total of no more than 20 officers and 247 Other Ranks. In five weeks they had lost, killed, wounded or missing, a total of 32 Officers and 714 Other Ranks.

This vicious fighting earned the Regiment three further battle honours: Aprilia, Carroceto and Italy 1943–44. It is sad, but understandable, that the number of battle honours to be carried on the Colours of any regiment had to be limited to ten (as in the Great War). Difficult choices had to be made after the war, and Anzio was selected as the 'generic' battle honour to cover this bloody episode in the Regiment's history.

There were no more reinforcements in Italy. Casualties in North Africa and at Anzio for the Irish Guards were as severe as they had been in the early stages of 1915. In the Second World War there was no possibility of completely rebuilding a Battalion more than once. This had happened after North Africa, ready for Italy. History repeats itself, for in 1918 the 2nd Battalion was removed to Criel Plage having ceased to be effective on account of constant heavy casualties. Then at Anzio the 1st Battalion's casualties were so severe, it too ceased to be an effective fighting Battalion for the remainder of the war.

Lt-Col Andrew Montagu-Douglas-Scott DSO. His father, already holder of a DSO, fought in South Africa with the Irish Guards Mounted Infantry Section. Colonel Andrew won his first DSO commanding the 1st Battalion and his second commanding a Brigade. His son also served in the 1st Battalion after the war. (Mercifully there was no war, so no DSOs, for the third generation.)

Medal, Italy Star. The Italy Star was awarded to those who fought in Italy at any time between 11 June 1943 and 8 May 1945. The colours of the ribbon represent the Italian colours. After the war a few soldiers of the North Irish Horse transferred to the Irish Guards. They, unusually, were permitted to wear a small maple leaf on the ribbon of the Italy Star, their regiment having served with distinction in a Canadian formation in Italy.

The survivors celebrated St Patrick's Day at Massalubrense near Sorrento where General Alex, after presenting Gallantry awards won at Anzio, distributed the Shamrock. Major Savill Young was awarded the DSO for Anzio. Like the Scotts, his father had served in the Great War, and his son followed the tradition. Capt H.F. McKinney; Quartermaster; General Alex; the Commanding Officer and Capt G.H. Willcocks, Director of Music.

Christmas in Italy. The Regimental Band performing at Foggia near Naples under the direction of Major George Willcocks (Director of Music 1938–1948).

The 1st Battalion was not to serve again in the Second World War. The survivors returned home to be absorbed into the other two service Battalions. Some, though, stayed in Italy. Foremost was Lt-Col Andrew Scott who was required to command 28th Infantry Brigade, and subsequently 1st Guards Brigade. Father Dolly became General Alex's Senior Religious Adviser. When General Alex went to call on the Pope in Rome he took Father Dolly with him. Waiting outside to be shown in to the presence, Father Dolly produced a small bakelite comb from his pocket. *'Dolly,'* said the General, *'how could you? Put it away!'*

The Warrant Officers of 1st Battalion Irish Guards. CSM Pestell; CSM Micky Moran; CSM Gilmore; CSM Stewart; CSM Paddy Mercer MM; D/Sgt Kenny; RSM McLoughlan; D/Sgt Bill Rooney MM; CSM George Stone.

Father Dolly Brookes

Surviving members of The 1st Battalion Irish Guards from Palestine in 1938 to Anzio in 1944.
Back Row: Gdsm. P McCarthy; Gdsm R. Adamson DCM; Gdsm J. Lavery; Gdsm P. O'Shea DCM; Gdsm J. Getbings; L/Sgt C. Englishby; Gdsm E. Davis; Gdsm E. Rooney; Gdsm E. Moore; L/Cpl D. Murphy; L/Cpl T. O'Connell; Gdsm J. Ryan MM.
Middle Row: Gdsm W. Gormley; Gdsm M. Lawton; Sgt A. Hughes MM; Sgt P. Hatche; Sgt M. McCarthy; L/Sgt C. Weir MM; L/Sgt P. McNally; L/Cpl R. Ashton; L/Sgt D. Smith; L/Sgt J. Sweeny; Gdsm S. Robinson; Gdsm G Prentice.
Front Row: L/Cpl S. Carr; Sgt R. McConnell MM; CQMS W. Wallace; CSM W. Pestell; D/Sgt M. Moran MM; Major D.M.L. Gordon-Watson MC; RSM W. Rooney MM; Major H.L.S. Young DSO; CSM G. Stone; Sgt O' Sullivan; L/Sgt P Freeman; L/Cpl G. Currie.

NORMANDY

Whilst waiting near Eastbourne to go to France, the 2nd and 3rd Battalions heard of the destruction of the Guards Chapel at the start of morning service on Sunday 18 June in which Major John Gilliatt and three other members of the Regiment were killed. Then on D+17 (23 June 1944) the first elements of the Guards Armoured Division sailed for France; the 3rd Battalion, with 'X' Company Scots Guards attached to make up numbers, in 32nd Guards (Lorried Infantry) Brigade the 2nd Armoured Battalion as part of 5th Guards Armoured Brigade. Before departure each troop was issued with a Firefly tank, a Sherman mounting an 18-pounder gun. Called a tank-buster it was a formidable weapon which was to prove its worth on many occasions in the months ahead.

En-route to France. Officers of 3rd Battalion. Lt Robin Hastings; Capt Desmond Kingsford (later MC, killed in Normandy); Major Ivo Reid and the Medical Officer.

The France and Germany Star was awarded to the Army for participation in any land operation in France, Belgium or Holland between 6 June 1944 and 8 May 1945. The colours of the ribbon are symbolic of the Union Flag and those of France and the Netherlands. The colours of Belgium could not be included in the ribbon, since they were the same as those of Germany.

Major 'Feathers' Steuart-Fotheringham, Company Commander of the redoubtable X Company Scots Guards. Note the Guards Armoured Division sign on the battle dress sleeve. This was a variation on the Great War design which was more stylised and on a different shield, showing the Ever Open Eye. After this design is named the Household Division yacht, *Gladeye*.

Taking part in a massive armoured thrust east of Cagny (OPERATION GOODWOOD), Lt John Gorman, a troop commander in 2nd Armoured Battalion was probing forward in his tank 'Ballyragget' when he suddenly found himself broadside on to a massive German tank which no one had ever seen before, the King Tiger. He fired one round from his 75mm gun which bounced off the German's armour. 'Ballyragget's gun then jammed, and seeing the beast's massive gun slowly traversing in his direction, John Gorman gave the order to ram.

'Ballyragget' struck the enemy amidships disabling the tank and causing its crew to bale out hurriedly. At this moment an artillery stonk came down.

After seeing his own crew to safety Lt Gorman commandeered a Firefly, 'Ballymena', whose commander had been killed, and completed the destruction of the King Tiger with his 18-pounder gun. He was awarded the MC, his driver, L/Cpl James Baron, an MM. The battle honour *Cagny* was awarded for the Regiment's part in OPERATION GOODWOOD.

These photographs were taken in early 1945 and were presented to the Irish Guards by Monsieur André Lechipey, who as a boy is seen sitting on the massive 88mm gun of the King Tiger, accompanied by his sister, with the disabled 'Ballyragget' in the foreground. Through diligent research members of the German tank crew were eventually identified and contacted in the 1990s and the existence of these photographs was discovered with the Germans providing the introduction to M. Lepichey.

Sergeant James Baron MM as a Chelsea Pensioner.

The first King Tiger Tank seen in battle. A photograph taken, we assume, nearer the time of the incident – the wireless aerials are intact.

In August the Guards Armoured Division was switched to the right of the British sector to exploit the penetration by 6th Guards Tank Brigade into the German defences at Point 309, christened Coldstream Hill after the exploits of the 4th Armoured Coldstream. Equipped with Churchill tanks they were able to deal with the massive high banks surrounding tiny fields that characterised the bocage country of Normandy – the only tanks that could do so.

Here, around the villages of St Martin des Besaces, St Charles de Percy and La Marvindière, the two Battalions of the Irish Guards suffered heavy casualties. The 3rd Battalion took part in a furious frontal attack down a forward slope at Sourdeval, under intense fire, as part of a brigade advance. Their losses were immense.

Around now 'X' Company Scots Guards left the 3rd Battalion. Theirs had been a successful and harmonious marriage and both sides were genuinely sad at parting. Their place was taken by an entire Number 4 Company created from the Mediterranean veterans of the 1st Battalion.

Few Micks who were in Normandy had ever heard of Mont Pinçon. It was the overall battle honour awarded for the first phase of the breakout from the Normandy landings bridgehead. It went to eight armoured regiments, two Yeomanry regiments, all five regiments of Foot Guards and to twenty-seven Infantry regiments.

Lt Hugh Dormer who was awarded the DSO for his remarkable undercover work in occupied France. After returning to his beloved 2nd Battalion he was killed in Normandy. In the last entry before D-Day in his recently republished diary – a moving testament by a deeply religious man – he wrote: '*God knows no man ever set out more happily or gladly before – and lead where it may, I follow the path in ever-mounting spirits. God grant me the courage not to let the Guardsmen down, knowing as I do how much they count on me. I only ask that He do with my life as He wills – if I should be privileged to give it on the field of battle, then indeed would the cup be full.*' Hugh Dormer was killed in a trivial incident in a Normandy orchard and as a brother officer wrote: '*He was buried with the others by the roadside and the Guardsmen came with bunches of flowers for his grave. They loved him because they knew he loved them.*'

Number One Company of the 3rd Battalion seen moving towards St Martin des Besaces accompanied by a Sherman of the 1st Armoured Coldstream, 2 August 1944. The second Guardsman carrying a shovel is Major Tony Brady, later the Regimental Archivist.

3rd Battalion's children's party at Montilly. Thirty local children were invited but in fact 110 turned up. When their guests were stuffed with food CSM Bill Gilchrist DCM organised Jeep rides.

Lt-Col J.O.E. Vandeleur, Commander Irish Guards Group. He was awarded two DSOs in North West Europe

At the end of August 1944, with both Battalions at Douai, a major reorganisation of Guards Armoured Division took place when Regimental Groups were formed each consisting of an infantry and an armoured Battalion of the same Regiment. Thus came into being the Irish Group. As senior commanding officer Lt-Col J.O.E. Vandeleur assumed overall command with his cousin, Lt-Col Giles Vandeleur, who had recently taken command of 2nd Armoured Battalion, remaining in command of the armour.

This marriage of infantry and tanks from the same regiment was to prove a battle-winning factor in the months ahead.

All 'spoke the same language', all had the same background and most had known each other all their military lives. There was perfect accord and complete mutual trust and the combination was to become renowned.

The Guards Armoured Division took no further part in the battles of Normandy. On 30 August they crossed the Seine amid growing fervour and increasing signs of enemy rout.

The evening after the new union Lt-Col J.O.E. gave out his first orders as Group Commander: *'The Irish Guards will dine in Brussels tomorrow night.'*

BRUSSELS

That night the crews worked until midnight and beyond. The distance to Brussels was little short of ninety miles. Would the engines, the tracks and the bogies take such punishment, let alone what nasty surprises a still determined enemy might have in store along the route?

Dawn on 3 September. A squadron of the Household Cavalry and the Welsh Guards Group pass through to take up the running. Then they were off. . .

'The 2nd Battalion had no mechanical trouble that day; for years they had been preparing their tanks for a day like this. Through the Belgian villages roared "St Patrick", "Ulster", "Leinster", and "Connaught", "Achill", "Bantry", "Cloneen" and sixty-seven other Irish villages and towns. The rattle of tank tracks on the cobbled streets brought the astonished inhabitants out of their houses to wave flags and cheer wildly . . . Opposition was by-passed or ignored.' (FitzGerald)

Amid a welcoming hail of hydrangeas and unripe apples the Irish Group reached the outskirts of Brussels around six o'clock.

Outskirts of Brussels. The crew of a Sherman of the 2nd Battalion beginning to sample the rapturous reception of Liberation. History repeated itself in Pristina, Kosovo in 1999.

The Liberation scenes in Brussels were soon a distant memory as the advance continued. Although supposedly in full retreat the German resistance was fierce and sometimes fanatical. North of the Albert Canal the enemy were, in great numbers, Panzer Regiments (brigades), SS Regiments and, nastiest of all, SS Panzers. To make matters worse the country was ill-suited to an armoured dash, a succession of broad canals or rivers, few bridges and these approached by narrow roads usually riding above the generally soggy landscape. On many occasions they were advancing on a single tank front with no means of getting off the road without getting bogged in the swampy ground.

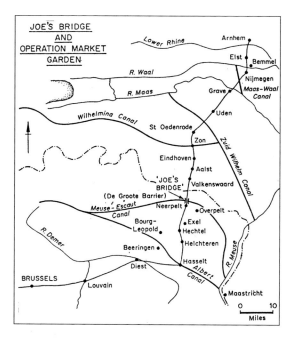

THE ATTACK ON JOE'S BRIDGE

On 10 September the wide-ranging reconnaissance scout cars of the invaluable 2nd Household Cavalry Regiment reported a brand new military road between Exel and Overpelt. More significantly, they reported that the bridge over the considerable Meuse-Escaut Canal at De Groote Barrier, although mined and strongly held by 88mm guns, was still intact.

Lt Desmond Lampard's troop of Shermans and the platoon of Lt John Stanley-Clarke were detailed to take the bridge under the covering fire of every tank in the Irish Group for they were beyond the range of any artillery support. It was nearly dark.

'It was after eight o'clock when the waiting crews saw the Very light burst green at the top of its arc (signal for maximum covering fire). Something or somebody had set fire to a large brick house on the right of the bridge. Whatever was inside it, it burnt remarkably well and the flames lit up the bridge and banks like a theatre set. For two minutes every gunner kept his foot hard down on the firing button that controlled his Browning machine-gun. All co-drivers who could see, and some who could not, fired their main guns. The red Very light went up (signal for the assault) and Lt Lampard's troop charged. In moments they were through and over the canal as were the platoon racing after them on either side of the bridge ignoring the fierce Spandau fire which broke around them. Then a very brave Sapper officer, Capt Hutton, with four Guardsmen, while bullets were rattling round them on the girders, removed the detonators from the charges. Capt Hutton was awarded the Military Cross, his four assistants Military Medals.' (FitzGerald)

Again and again the Germans tried to regain the bridge whose capture had so unpinned their defence; again and again they were beaten off.

The bridge over the Meuse-Escaut Canal at De Groote Barrier is now named 'JOE's Bridge' in honour of its captor.

Right: **The taking of JOE's Bridge.**

Left: **Memorial to the Irish Guards Battle Group at JOE's Bridge.**

Breakout from the Escaut Canal Bridgehead. 2nd Battalion tanks advancing across the Escaut Canal over the Bailey bridge constructed beside the original JOE's Bridge captured intact on 10 September.

Infantry cross by JOE's Bridge.

The remains of a German 88 mm which had once defended it. These powerful guns were also used in the lower register in an anti-tank role.

MARKET GARDEN

With JOE's Bridge secured on 14 September, they pulled back to regroup at Overpelt. Here they learned of OPERATION MARKET GARDEN. The 'Market' element was an airborne assault by the Americans on Nijmegen, the bridge over the massive Mass-Waal Canal, and the River Waal itself, and that of the British 6th Airborne Division further on at Arnhem. 'Garden' was the link up by ground forces. The Irish Group were given the dubious honour of leading the latter.

NEERPELT

Consolidating in the main square of Valkenswaard before resuming the advance. At that stage, Allied air superiority was total so 'bunching' was not such a sin as it had been.

NIJMEGEN

Following close on the American airborne assault on Nijmegen, the bridge over the River Waal was stormed and captured intact by the Grenadier Group. On 21 September the Irish Group passed through and took over its defence.

The purpose of OPERATION GARDEN was for the ground troops to link up with the Airborne Division which was gallantly holding Arnhem. It proved to be impossible to link up in time because of the very narrow front and strong resistance. [This is the origin of the expression 'A Bridge too Far', later the title of an American epic film to the intense irritation of those who had participated in 1944. The only entertainment was that Colonel J.O.E. Vandeleur was played by Michael Caine, with whom he got on famously.] The Irish Guards Group managed to link with the US 101st Airborne Division at Zon, and reached Nijmegen. They were awarded a further battle honour, *Aam,* for the actions of 1–4 October 1944 clearing eastwards up the River Maas.

The Divisional Commander, Major-General Sir Allan Adair, who led the Guards Armoured Division with such distinction, inspects the warrant officers of the 3rd Battalion somewhere in Holland. Watching, the Commanding Officer, Lt-Col Dennis Fitzgerald and Adjutant; D/Sgt 'Tommo' Thompson; D/Sgt Jack Thackrah MM; CSM 'Johnno' Johnstone DCM; Capt Jimmy Quinn.

Above: **A Sherman of the 2nd Battalion** consolidates the position.

Right: **A 6-pounder anti-tank gun**, 20 September, at the approaches to Nijmegen road bridge. Quiet reigns and a Guardsman has his hair cut.

Meeting up with the American 101st Airborne Division on 18 September at Zon, north of Eindhoven where the bridge across the massive Wilhelmina Canal had been destroyed.

Nearing the end in Germany. Shermans in a typical German village. Surrender was imminent.

Gdsm Edward Charlton VC. (For full citation see p. 210)

Mrs Charlton, Gdsm Charlton's mother, on 28 May 1956 presenting her son's Victoria Cross to the Regiment.

NEARING THE END

The battle now moved across the Rhine into Germany, meeting furious resistance from fanatical German defenders. The honour *Hochwald* was awarded for the 2nd and 3rd Battalions' fighting between 24 February and 4 March 1945. Similarly awards were made for the *Rhine*, 25 March – 1 April 1945, and *Bentheim*, 2–3 April 1945.

On 21 April, while probing forward by the village of Wistedt near the town of Elsdorf, a troop of Shermans and its supporting platoon were caught in a German counter-attack. With his tank disabled Gdsm Edward Charlton, the co-driver, dismounted his Browning machine-gun in full view of the enemy and advanced firing from the hip to cover the withdrawal of the remainder of the little force. Wounded in the arm he propped the gun on a gate and continued to fire with the other until, hit again, he fell. Despite every effort of the German doctors he later died of his wounds.

This incredible deed was unrecognised until a Guardsman who had temporarily been taken prisoner escaped to tell what had happened. This was later confirmed by a captured German officer who, like his men, had been astonished by the Guardsman's courage.

Gdsm Edward Charlton was posthumously awarded the Victoria Cross, the last in Europe during the Second World War.

RHINELAND

Victory Parade, Luxembourg, May 1945. His Royal Highness Prince Felix of Luxembourg; Her Royal Highness the Grand Duchess Charlotte of Luxembourg; Prince Jean Hereditary Grand Duke of Luxembourg, Lieutenant Irish Guards and since 1984, Colonel of the Regiment.
The Irish Guards contingent led by CSM Jock Monks with, *L–R:*, Sgt George Hare and Sgt J. Cain MM.

War Medal. Awarded to all full time servicemen who had completed 28 days' service before 2 September 1945.

Brigadier Derek Mills-Robert DSO, MC* was in the Supplementary Reserve of Officers before the war. After serving with the 1st Battalion in Norway, he transferred to the Commandos. He commanded 6 Commado in North Africa (1943) and then 1st Commando Brigade in North-west Europe. For many years he chaired the North of England Branch of the Irish Guards Association.

THE END

On 29 June 1945, at Rotenburg Airfield in Germany, the Guards Armoured Division paraded for the last time with their armour. At 11.30 Field Marshal Montgomery arrived and, after inspecting the parade in a half-track, took his place on the saluting base.

Then the columns of tanks advanced and counter-marched across the ground, each tank commander traversing his turret and saluting. The columns turned and swung away over the hills in the background. As they disappeared the bands broke into the strains of 'Auld Lang Syne'.

There followed a short pause. Then coming over the crest of the hill could be seen the marching columns of the former armoured Battalions. To their regimental marches played in succession by the bands, they came striding down the arena to join their comrades of the Foot Guards below.

As the old familiar tunes rang out what memories must have been stirred in those present that day! Of Cagny; of the costly fighting in the Bocage; of the welcome on the gallop to Brussels; of the great liberation scenes themselves; of the Escaut Canal, MARKET GARDEN and the bitter fighting before reaching Germany. Of individual acts – John Gorman's ramming of the King Tiger in Normandy; Desmond Lampard's dash at JOE's Bridge and Gdsm Charlton's incredible personal battle for which the Victoria Cross had just been announced. And memories of so many more whose endurance and example and skill at arms had added one more passage to the fighting record of the Regiment.

In the Second World War the Irish Guards lost in all 734 dead, including fifty-nine officers. They were awarded two Victoria Crosses; seventeen DSOs; eighteen DCMs; thirty-three MCs and seventy-two MMs.

The Farewell to Armour Parade.

After the war the bombed Guards Chapel was rebuilt. Each regiment now has its own memorial chapel and altar. On the Irish Guards altar is a small silver Cross of Moone which stands on an altar cloth personally designed by Field Marshal Alex. In the cloister of the Guards Chapel is the Regimental book of remembrance. And to the Guards Memorial, facing Horse Guards Parade, the scene of peacetime glory, has been added a modest commemoration of those who gave their lives in the Second World War and in campaigns thereafter.

CHAPTER FIVE

1946–1965

POST WAR YEARS

In 1946 the remnants of the 3rd Battalion were incorporated into the 1st and a few months later the 2nd Battalion was once more placed in suspended animation. Prior to that, the 1st Battalion had been sent to Palestine to help keep some semblance of peace between Jews and Arabs before the British Mandate expired

This was the most intense Internal Security situation yet experienced. So it was with mixed feelings that, in company with the other British forces, the Battalion pulled out in June 1948.

An all-too-short few months in Tripoli were succeeded by home service until, in 1951, they found themselves in Germany at Hubbelrath near Dusseldorf with 4th Guards Brigade.

1953 was Coronation Year and to the Regiment's great pride, a picked contingent, brought back from Germany, provided the Guard of Honour outside Buckingham Palace.

The German tour ended in 1953 and was immediately succeeded by a spell in the Canal Zone in Egypt before home service took over again for several years. 1958 was interrupted by four months active service in Cyprus including security operations against EOKA.

With heightening East-West tension, the regiment found itself in 1961 at the heart of the Cold War, in West Germany.

Returning in 1964 to a rebuilt Chelsea Barracks, apart from Battalion training in Libya, public duties absorbed their time.

**1st Battalion Irish Guards,
Nefisha Football Ground, Canal Zone,
Egypt, 1955. Commanding Officer,
Lt-Col H.L.S. Young** DSO.

Amalgamation of the Officers of 1st and 3rd Battalions, 20 August 1946.
Back Row: 2/Lt G. Rooney; 2/Lt M.H. Vernon; 2/Lt G.B.A.F. Rowell; 2/Lt M. Levine; Lt M.E.H. Mullholland; 2/Lt M.N. Garnett; 2/Lt M.C. Robinson; Lt C.K. Atkins; Lt P.A. Filmer-Sankey; 2/Lt Martin;
Middle Row: 2/Lt T.C.P. Whidbourne; Lt A.I.S Boyd; Lt T.Crowe; Capt R.D.C. Bacon; Lt A.S. Reid; Capt M.J. de R. Richardson; Lt B.S. Dale; Lt A.C.B. Millar; Capt J.C. Crewe MC; Capt J.V. Taylor MC; *Seated:* Capt G. Gordon-Shee; Capt P.A. McCall; Capt P.C.H. Pollock; Major D.H. FitzGerald DSO; Colonel C.A. Montagu-Douglas-Scott DSO; Major J.D. Hornung OBE MC; Major H.L.S. Young DSO; Major A Bell MC; Capt (QM) J. Keating MBE.

In October 1946 a detached company moved to Hillsborough, the first time the Regiment had been stationed in Northern Ireland.

Inspection of the Governor's Guard by His Excellency The Earl Granville, Governor-General of Northern Ireland.

Guard Mounting at Buckingham Palace in battledress, February 1947. Note the presence of the subaltern of the St James's Palace detachment (later dispensed with) as well as the subaltern of the Buckingham Palace detachment. The Guard wears great coats and woollen gloves, with service dress caps. The 1938 pattern webbing braces are being worn outside the great coats, and the officers carry a .38 pistol in a webbing holster on the right side. Web anklets were worn, a custom which later ceased in Battalions in London District and at the Guards Depot.

The Colours of the 2nd Battalion being marched on to parade for the last time. The only occasion upon which a warrant officer carries two Colours.

Laying up the Colours of the 2nd Battalion at Colchester, July 1947. *L–R:* Capt J.D. Chichester-Clarke (later Prime Minister of Northern Ireland); Major J.D. Hornung OBE, MC, Regimental Adjutant; Lt-Col B.O.P. Eugster DSO, MC, Commanding Officer; Colonel J.O.E. Vandeleur DSO, Regimental Lieutenant Colonel; Capt P. Foden Patterson; Capt A.G. Reid.

PALESTINE

In the spring of 1947 the 1st Battalion was once again in Palestine. This time its role was to preside over the expiring Mandate and to attempt to keep Jew and Arab apart – so being heartedly disliked by both sides. The ensuing months saw the most bitter and intensive Internal Security operations ever undertaken by British forces up to that time.

Enforcing the curfew in Haifa, 15–18 April 1947.

Jerusalem, 28 July–30 September 1947. Search of Givat Shaul.

Left: **House searching.**

Right: **Arms cache found under a stone wall.**

Left: **Road block.**

Right: **A load of straw looks suspect.**

GSM Palestine 1945–48.

Rosh Pinna, St Patrick's Day 1948. *L–R:* CSM Smart; the Quartermaster, Capt J. ('K') Keating MBE; Sgt 'Maxie' McComish MM.

Presiding over the affairs of the 1st Battalion, as he had those of the 2nd Battalion during the War, was the Quartermaster, Capt Jack 'K' Keating. A native of Ballyragget in County Kilkenny he was a man of infinite charm and instant wit. The name Ballyragget has a place of its own in the Regiment. In a David and Goliath action, a tank of that name rammed a giant King Tiger. Keating's son also joined the Regiment as a Guardsman and like his father achieved a commission.

L–R: **CQMS Jack Pestell; CSM Paddy Mercer** MM; **CSM Micky Moran** MM; **RSM George Howe.**

Battalion sports at Rosh Pinna. The Commanding Officer, Lt-Col D.H. FitzGerald DSO, competing in the bicycle race.

The Battalion unofficial mascot 'Capstar' with Capt Bill Churchill.

Donkey Power. CSM Jack Pestell giving encouragement.

The pipers playing at Safad, an area of some risk. Unusually, the Drum Major leads the pipes, and the pipers' bonnets are worn at an angle that is no longer fashionable.

After a lapse of nearly ten years, in 1949 the Brigade of Guards returned to tunic and bearskin.

The first guard to be mounted by the Regiment at HM Tower of London in full dress, 15 May 1949. The Drum Major, for whom no gold-laced Drum Major's tunic was available from the pre-war stock, is wearing a warrant officer's tunic with the four large inverted chevrons of the Drum Major's appointment on his sleeve.

Preparation, Kings Birthday Parade, 1949. Sgt F. Beattie and Gdsm P. Duffy (later Major Pat Duffy MBE).

In July 1949 a serious national dock strike saw the Battalion working in the docks. Unskilled men could never match the performance of the experienced dockers, so ran the theory. The Guardsmen, enjoying the novelty and relishing the opportunity to prove a point, astonished the port authorities by the speed at which they were able to unload huge tonnages with relative ease.

Fiftieth Anniversary, St Patrick's Day 1950.

The Golden Jubilee Ball. In keeping with tradition, a dance programme was produced.

A well decorated group. RSM Bill Rooney MM (Palestine 1938); D/Sgt Micky Moran MM (Anzio 1943) and D/Sgt 'Johnno' Johnstone DCM (Norway 1940).

An aerial view of the march past at Chelsea Barracks after the distribution of the Shamrock by His Majesty King George VI.

Presentation of Colours, 27 July 1949 at Buckingham Palace. The King is seen talking to the Colonel of the Regiment. *L–R:* Lt-Col T.E.G. Nugent MVO, MC; Major P.F.I. Reid, Regimental Adjutant; Capt the Lord Plunkett, Equerry; The Colonel of the Regiment; The King; Colonel T.W. Gimson, Regimental Lieutenant Colonel. Two of the Ensigns who carried the Colours, Pat and Micky (late Archbishop of Southwark) Bowen, were sons of John Bowen, killed on the *Chobry*. The Colours presented on this occasion displayed only the honours awarded for the Great War. The battle honours awarded to the Regiment for its service in the Second World War were authorised in 1956, and only then were honours added to the Colours. On the King's Colour they were set in two columns of ten, one on each side of the central device. On the Regimental Colour the twenty honours were arranged in two columns of five on each lateral arm of the cross. These are now in the Guards Chapel.

Field Marshal The Rt Hon the Earl Alexander of Tunis and Errigal in the County of Donegal KG, PC, GCB, OM, GCMG, CSI, DSO, MC, Colonel of the Regiment (1946–1969), then Minister of Defence, lays the Regimental wreath at the Guards Memorial, 1952.

Contingent from the Battalion for the funeral of His Majesty King George VI, 1952. Sixteen officers were brought back to London to form one watch for the Lying in State of King George VI. Officers of the Household Division share with the Queen's Bodyguard of the Gentlemen-at-Arms and the Queen's Bodyguard of the Yeomen of the Guard the privilege of guarding the coffin of the Sovereign continuously while it lies in state in Westminster Hall. Each period of twenty-four hours is divided into four watches of six hours. Each watch consists of a minimum of sixteen officers and the Officer Commanding the watch (not below the rank of Lieutenant Colonel). Four officers are on duty together round the coffin, and two officers are always in waiting, of whom one stands at the top landing of the steps and one remains dressed and ready for duty if called upon. (Standing Orders for the Brigade of Guards, 1952).

The Regimental Band playing in the City Hall Grounds, Belfast, after the Coronation under Major C.H. 'Jigs' Jaeger OBE, Director of Music 1948–1969.

Coronation of Her Majesty Queen Elizabeth II, 2 June 1953. Guard of Honour found by 1st Battalion Irish Guards outside Buckingham Palace. *L–R:* Capt C.W.D. Harvey-Kelly; 2/Lt J.E.L. Nugent; Lt R.A.C. Plummer.

THE CANAL ZONE, EGYPT

From 1954 to 1956 the Battalion formed part of the British Garrison in the Canal Zone, Egypt.

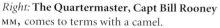

Above: **Sons and grandsons** of former members of the Regiment serving in the Canal Zone in 1955.

Left: **The Queen's Birthday Parade, Moascar,** June 1954. Regimental Sergeant Major Micky Moran MM, with drawn sword, receives the Regimental Colour before handing it over to the Ensign. Note the use of the Regimental Colour on a parade when the Sovereign is not present.

Right: **The Quartermaster, Capt Bill Rooney MM,** comes to terms with a camel.

Berwick Camp, Fanara. Company Lines.

CHRISTMAS DAY 1955

Left: **The Sergeants' Mess Team arrives by trailer train towed by an Austin Champ.** Christmas was traditionally celebrated overseas in the pre-television age, with an Officers v Sergeants football match and sports. Every subterfuge was employed to ensure a Sergeants' Mess victory, and the atmosphere was mischievous. The Officers always claimed to have 'been robbed!'.

Stella (Beer) Cup.

The two teams, and assorted hangers-on. In the picture: Tony Ross (lying in front); Maxie McComish (in galibeah); Ibrahim, the Sudanese cook; Keith Thomas; Major Mark White; Capt Tony Plummer, Adjutant; Major Stephen Langton, Second-in-Command; Capt John Ghika; Lt Richard Barrow; Major Bobby O'Grady; Lt-Col Savill Young, Commanding Officer; Tom Barry; Harry Fanning; Nobby Clarke; Jimmy Wilde, ORQMS; Major Paddy Grogan; Capt Denis Grehan; D/Sgt Dai Evans; Dan Moriarty; Martin Campbell; Philip Lucas; Capt John Head; Tom Gaffney.

After the Commanding Officer was tackled by D/Sgt Dai Evans, in a moment of forgetfulness that he was now playing soccer, things became confused.

Over the first fence in the 1955 Grand National. The Assistant Regimental Adjutant, Major Mike MacEwan, rides 'Minimax' (32). 'Royal Tan' (2) was the eventual winner.

Irish Guards Boys, Pirbright, November 1955. The front rank includes: CQMS Ramsey; Lt Jan van Moyland; Major Tony Aylmer; CSM 'Tabs' Mahoney; Sgt Donnan; L/Cpl Mallinson.

Boy soldiers had originally been trained as drummers or tailors and were under the guidance of the Adjutant and the Drum Major of the Battalions of Foot Guards. When Battalions went abroad the boys were sent to the Training Battalion at Pirbright. After the Second World War more opportunities for junior entry into the Army became available, so the Foot Guards set up a Boys' Company (later re-named the Junior Guardsmen's Company) at Pirbright. The age of enlistment never went below 15½. Juniors received education and specialist training before graduating to the Guards Depot at the age of 17½. They were trained as drummers, pipers, clerks, grooms, tailors and signallers.

Another stream of Junior Leaders, enlisted with higher educational qualifications, was trained at Oswestry (and later Shorncliffe) in the Guards Junior Leaders (Waterloo) Company, part of the Infantry Junior Leaders Battalion. The success of junior training was spectacular. It yielded a high proportion of the most successful warrant and non-commissioned officers. With the re-organisation of training resulting from Options for Change in 1991, adult training was re-structured and the Guards Depot, most regrettably, came to an end. Junior Guardsmen and Junior Leaders ceased to be trained, and the Household Division lost a valuable source of high-grade manpower.

CYPRUS

In 1958, when stationed at Shorncliffe in Kent and without warning, the Battalion was placed at seven-days' notice to move … somewhere …

… This turned out to be Cyprus, for once again the Middle East was in turmoil. On arrival the Battalion was deployed in company groups in the rural areas around the capital, Nicosia, with close support from the armoured cars of The Royal Horse Guards (The Blues). The EOKA campaign was still active with atrocities between Greek and Turk a daily occurrence. Cordon and search operations became commonplace.

Above: **Number One Company rounding up suspects.** The 1st Guards Brigade sign showing the 'Ever Open Eye' can be seen on the Land Rover.

Left: **Identification of suspects.** RSM Paddy Mercer MM visiting the cage.

Below and bottom right: **Support Company on a Brigade Exercise in the Panhandle.** The anti-tank platoon equipped with the 120mm Mobat which had replaced the venerable 17-pounder.

Medal GSM Cyprus.

Under guard in makeshift cages.

ST PATRICK'S DAY

The Shamrock arrives courtesy Aer Lingus.

Father and son. The Colonel of the Regiment, Field Marshal Alex and 2/Lt The Hon. Brian Alexander.

L/Cpl G. Murphy fixing the Shamrock to the hat of his grandfather, Chelsea Pensioner Sgt S.C. Murphy DCM, a veteran of the Boer War. The wearing of Service Dress Caps ceased in 1958.

L/Cpl Dodd gives the Shamrock to his daughter. He is wearing two long service chevrons, the crossed flags of a B3 signaller and the Cyprus General Service Medal

ST PATRICK'S DAY

Three cheers for Her Royal Highness The Princess Royal, Windsor 1960. Capt Peter Thomas in front and Sgt Ambrose Latham nearest the camera.

Her Royal Highness The Princess Royal presents Shaun with his Shamrock, Caterham 1961. The Royal gift has been presented annually since 1901 – firstly by Queen Alexandra until her death in 1925; then by Princess Mary, later to become The Princess Royal, until 1964. In 1964 Queen Elizabeth The Queen Mother, who first attended St Patrick's Day in 1927, began her long era of presenting the Shamrock – very often in person despite the frequent conflict over dates with Cheltenham Races.

Company Commanders receiving the Shamrock for their companies from the Colonel of the Regiment, Chelsea 1965. *L–R:* Capt 'Johnno' Johnstone MBE, DCM, Quartermaster; the Colonel of the Regiment; Major G.A. Allan; Major P.V. Verney; CSM George Shannon; Major J.N. Ghika. In this photograph the Colonel is distributing the Shamrock presented by the Queen Mother.

On a visit to the United States in 1960 a battered Great War bugle was presented to the 69th National Guard Regiment (The Fighting 69th). This Irish regiment had served beside the Irish Guards in the Great War. RQMS Victor Sullivan, Major Giles Allan and Lt-Col Lynch of the Fighting 69th.

Snow at Windsor. A photographic opportunity. 2/Lt Paul de Remusat takes the officer's patrol at Windsor. This is one of a series of posed photographs taken for the 1960 Christmas card. Eventually a picture showing the drummer carrying a lantern was selected.

Guard of Honour at HM Tower of London for the installation of the Colonel of the Regiment as Constable of the Tower of London. His son Brian was the Ensign. 1960.

The old .303 Lee Enfield No 4 Rifle which had served so well for so long was succeeded by the 7.62mm Self Loading Rifle which required a different drill.

The Guards Depot moved from Caterham, its home for years, to Pirbright in 1960.

Review of the Household Troops on the occasion of the State Visit of President de Gaulle. In the Irish Guards contingent were Major William Harvey-Kelly; Capt James Baker; Lt Anthony Wordsworth; Lt Donough O'Brien and 2/Lt the Hon Brian Alexander. RSM Arthur Bell of 1st Battalion Irish Guards was correctly identified by General de Gaulle as the smartest man on parade. The Battalion smiled quietly to itself and wondered what General de Gaulle knew about drill.

Left: **Drum Major Keith Thomas** BEM marches off the Old Guard, Shaun and Gdsm Birmingham leading.

Below: **In 1961 the Battalion returned to Dusseldorf** as part of the British Army of the Rhine. This was the first air trooping to Germany by the British Army and was from the newly opened Gatwick Airport. There were not enough married quarters at Hubbelrath for the over strength and heavily married Battalion. So the Commanding Officer, Lt-Col Stephen Langton MVO, MC, decided to solve the problem. To the consternation of the authorities, he somehow obtained a fleet of mobile-home-style caravans which were parked in a back area of the barracks, thus enabling numerous families to be united. It was a good idea; but the climate in winter was not too good. The gesture put a great spark into the powers that were, and soon the quartering situation was resolved.

Below: **On the way to Gatwick.** CSM Jimmy Officer; Shaun; Sgt Ambrose Latham; 2/Lt Willie Mahon.

Champion of Crufts, Shaun, with his handler Gdsm Birmingham.

In 1960 Capt John Oakes, Army and Combined Services downhill champion for the previous two years, was chosen to captain the British Ski Team at the Winter Olympics in Squaw Valley, California.

Sgt Lally with the MOBAT anti-tank gun, training at Sennelager. This was the era of each rifle company having its own support platoon.

C/Sgt Martin Aldridge (a keen amateur photographer and uncle of Major Pat Duffy) is seen here at Vogelsang (a Belgian run training area in the Eifel Mountains) in 'Palmerstown', the Pioneer Commander's APC. The Battalion was equipped with the Humber 1 Ton Armoured, otherwise known as the 'Pig'. Underpowered on account of the armour, and weak in the clutch, the vehicle had a reputation for breaking down and bogging in. The Battalion generated extraordinary hysteria over the loss of red glass tail covers, known as rubies. Commanding Officer's vehicle inspections became a fruitful money spinner for the less scrupulous purveyors of spare rubies.

Companies named their vehicles on a system derived from the 2nd Battalion's tanks, a custom which continues.

TRAINING IN GERMANY

Bren shoot. *L–R:* Gdsm O'Reilly; L/Cpl Deegan; Gdsm Lawless; L/Sgt Megaw; Lt Robert Corbett.

ennelager 1961.

THE GUARDS DEPOT

With the end of National Service in 1960, it became necessary to consolidate the training arrangements of the Foot Guards. The Guards Depot had been in the grim barracks at Caterham since the previous century. Mecca of military standards, it contained a company from each regiment. Rivalry was friendly, but acute. No 5 Company Irish Guards occupied Roberts and Alexander blocks, and had their own cook house. The company was fully staffed by Irish Guards NCOs and Trained Soldiers (who wore a brass Brigade Star on the right arm to distinguish them from recruits). Training (drill, weapon training and physical training) took twenty-four weeks. Thereafter recruits became Trainee Guardsmen and moved to Pirbright to the Guards Training Battalion. This was run on similar lines to Caterham, but the emphasis was on field training. No 7 Company Irish Guards undertook all continuation and tactical training for the Regiment. There was a Battle camp in Pickering in Yorkshire.

In 1960 the Guards Depot closed at Caterham and moved to Pirbright. The tactical types from the Training Battalion said it would be all drill and no tactics. The drill people thought standards would never be the same again. The Training Battalion vanished for ever. And the Guards Depot became a stronger, more all-round, magnificently equipped organisation, fulfilling the most demanding training needs to perfection.

This period saw the re-introduction of the wartime policy of cross postings of companies and platoons of the Household Division. Just as X Company Scots Guards had been so special to the 3rd Battalion Irish Guards during the Normandy Campaign so the exchanges began anew.

Number Three Company was detached to join 2nd Battalion Scots Guards in Kenya. The Company marches past the commanding officer Lt-Col Stephen Langton MVO, MC. The Company Commander, Major Tony Plummer is followed by CSM George Shannon.

In 1965, after a gap of 44 years, the Battalion won the Army Athletics Championship as well as being London District Athletic and Cross Country Champions, Eastern Command Athletic and Cross Country Champions, Lawson Cup and Prince of Wales Relay Race winners. *Back row:* Gdsm Doyle; Gdsm Raley; Musn Ashford; Gdsm Hayden; Gdsm Fearon; Gdsm McManus; Gdsm Herriott; Gdsm Wishart; L/Cpl McDonagh; Gdsm Little; L/Cpl Gilpin; L/Cpl Lockhart; unidentified.

Centre row: Gdsm O'Sullivan; Gdsm Parry; Gdsm Mooney; Gdsm Harper; L/Cpl Turner; Gdsm Graham; Gdsm MacDonald; L/Cpl Byrne; Gdsm Hanlon; Gdsm Stone; Gdsm Kewley; L/Sgt McKinty *Front row:* Sgt Dent, A.P.T.C.; Lt R.C. Wolverson; Sgt MacDermot; Capt The Viscount Cole; L/Sgt Murphy; Lt-Col C.W.D. Harvey-Kelly; L/Sgt Cleary; Major G.A. Allan; L/Sgt Green; 2/Lt A.N. Foster; RSM Steuart.

No 4 Company was re-numbered as No 9 and joined 1st Battalion Scots Guards as part of the Commonwealth Brigade in Terendak, Malacca, Malaysia. After jungle training in Johore Bahru the Battalion deployed on the first of two roulement tours to Borneo, by then part of Malaysia. Operations consisted of setting up company bases in the jungle and undertaking long active service patrols in defence of the Malaysian border which was being 'confronted' by frequent raids by the Indonesian Army.

Above: **Borneo,** February 1965. Returning from patrol, Padawan, Sarawak. *L–R:* Gdsm Donley; Sgt Johnston; Gdsm Fleming.

Right: **Campaign Service Medal.** Clasps Malay Peninsula, Borneo.

Below: **Borneo, 1965. L/Sgt Carvill briefs his patrol.** *L–R:* Gdsm Johnson; Gdsm Maxwell. *Rear Row:* Gdsm Butterworth (later Capt Colin Butterworth); Gdsm Connolly 36. (After active service in the Congo with the Irish Army he was one of several soldiers who later served in the Irish Guards and wore the UN Congo Medal. Needless to say he was universally known as 'Congo Joe').

Above: **Borneo,** 1965. Building a helicopter pad in the jungle. *L–R:* Gdsm Millar, Mackrell, Spencer, Johnson, Montgomery, L/Sgt Moore and Mitchell.
This was at the height of the Vietnam War when helicopter tactics tried by the US Army revolutionised rapid reaction in jungle warfare.

Right: **Padawan Camp, Sarawak.** Gun pits in the company lines. The guns are 105mm Pack Howitzers of 6 (Light) Regiment Royal Artillery based at Terendak.

LIBYA, 1965

1st Battalion Irish Guards based in Chelsea Barracks found itself, somewhat improbably, offered a break from public duties in the form of a Battalion exercise in the Libyan desert. The Battalion's transport had an adventurous trip by road via Italy and thence by sea to Tobruk.

The remainder of the Battalion flew by RAF Transport Command to El Adem, a huge RAF base not far from the Egyptian border. Surprisingly all went more or less according to plan.

On arrival each company was driven for some distance along the coast road towards Derna, to an unlovely spot called Timimi. There, in widely spaced out locations, training went on, ending with several days of what were known as Battalion stunts.

It was proper, rough old 8th Army desert, and minefields and the odd unexploded grenade were still in evidence. So were occasional locals who appeared out of nowhere to sell miserable, small eggs to voracious Guardsmen who were not impressed, and said so, in the time honoured fashion ... 'IMSHI!' Desert navigation was at best hazardous for a public duties Battalion, whether in transport, or on foot. But somehow supplies always reached the companies.

A 1965 nominal roll of the Battalion for emplaning purposes reveals over 85% Irish addresses for the next of kin.

Three scenes in Libya. **No 1 Company Base Camp.** *Top:* **L/Sgt Cushion erects a bivouac.** *Centre:* **Company base camp.** *Bottom:* **Drummer Deane (later Drum Major Dixie Deane BEM)** and Gdsm Jimmy Hayden, heavyweight boxer, with members of No. 1 Company. At this stage battle dress (BD) had been replaced by Combat dress, but puttees had not yet replaced 1938 pattern web anklets. New Boots DMS (Directly Moulded Sole) had just been introduced, but some still wore Boots CWW (Cold Wet Weather, known as 'Boots Cobbly Wobbly'). Berets remained dark blue, except in the case of one or two senior officers who had served in the 3rd Battalion during the war, who wore brown berets.

Early morning cordon and search operation, (Aden 1967).

CHAPTER SIX

1966–1985

END OF EMPIRE

This period covers the end of residual imperial responsibilities. The Regiment, at its peacetime establishment of a single Battalion, deployed more frequently and to more different theatres than ever before.

In the Far East, No 9 company continued to serve in East and West Malaysia with 1st Bn Scots Guards until 1967, while the Battalion itself was in Hong Kong for two and a half years from late 1971. In 1965 an affiliation was cemented with 4th Battalion The Royal Australian Regiment which led to several excellent Australian officers later serving with the 1st Battalion Irish Guards, especially in British Army of the Rhine.

In the Middle East the Battalion was involved in the uncomfortable and scrappy Aden wind down (1966–1967).

In Africa the Battalion sent monitoring parties to Rhodesia in 1980, as well as a company exercise to Ghana (during 1978).

There were infantry exercises in Canada at Winnipeg and mechanised exercises in Alberta at British Army Training Unit Suffield. Operational tours also took place at intervals in the jungles of Belize.

In Europe the Cold War ebbed and flowed, with the Battalion taking its full mechanised part in BAOR, in 4th Guards Brigade at Munster (which, in what was perceived as a gesture to appease a 'high up', was re-named 4 Armoured Brigade in 1977).

At home public duties were still maintained at the usual immaculate level. Duties in aid of the Civil Power emerged in the form of OPERATION BURBERRY, firefighting in London during the national firemen's strike, using the venerable Green Goddess, as well as standby duties for London Flooding (OPERATION GIRAFFE!) and Heathrow Airport emergencies.

Such were the balmy days of peace.

Presentation of Colours, 10 June 1966, Buckingham Palace.

March past with the new Colours.
L–R: Colour Point (marker) C/Sgt Allister. *On the steps:* Lt-Col Tony Aylmer,
Commanding Officer; Field Marshal The Earl Alexander of Tunis (Colonel of the
Regiment); Lt-Col The Lord Patrick Plunkett (Irish Guards, Equerry to Her Majesty);
Colonel William Harvey-Kelly (Regimental Lieutenant Colonel), and Her Majesty.
The Colour Party *L–R:* 2/Lt Robin Bullock-Webster with the Queen's Colour (Crimson);
C/Sgt George Fawcett, and 2/Lt Charles Aikenhead with the Regimental Colour.

ADEN

No sooner was the Birthday Parade over, and the new Colours were paraded for the first time, when training for Aden began in earnest. This included a Battalion exercise among the sheep at Sennybridge in Wales (a great setting for Arabian urban or mountain operations for which they were preparing!). Nowadays it seems astonishing that a public duties Battalion should be sent with minimal preparations to a place like Aden, where the operational situation was difficult and about to explode. It was a busy time.

The Battalion formed part of 24 Brigade (as it had been in Norway in 1940) and was based in Salerno Camp, Little Aden near the huge smelly BP refinery. Aden, once a crucial British coaling station on the route to India, had been struggling for independence. In 1966 the British government, keen to be rid of troublesome colonies, announced the date for independence to be late 1967. This was the signal for violence throughout the South Arabian Federation, as it had become. Power hungry rival armed groups, both of which hated the British, fought running battles with each other for power. They were FLOSY (Front for the Liberation of South Yemen), and the NLF (National Liberation Front). The Battalion, which relieved 1st Bn Welsh Guards, had an action packed tour.

No sooner had they arrived than they found themselves on OPERATION FATE, an amphibious landing down the coast of East Aden Protectorate at a guerilla training camp. This resulted in a number of suspects being detained and many illegal weapons confiscated.

OPERATION FATE. No 3 Company formed up, wearing life jackets, waiting to land at Hauf from HMS *Fearless*. At front right wearing a beret is 2/Lt Anthony Weldon and at the very back, on the left, Pipe Major Tom Ramsey's bonnet can be seen. He was the third Ramsey to be the Pipe Major.

OPERATION FATE. Suspects awaiting questioning are held in the compound erected by the Pioneer Platoon. In the background a landing craft from HMS *Fearless*.

Patrolling and Internal Security duties in Aden occupied much of their time. Here 2/Lt David Carleton-Paget and Sgt Jim Driscoll with close support from a Land Rover are all alertness in Ma'alla, a notorious district in what was known as Big Aden.

The Battalion had its own air platoon under direct command for the first time. It consisted of three Sioux recce helicopters, one flown by Capt Garry Daintry (seen here over the Radfan), the others by Foot Guards officers on loan.

There were also tours of duty up country at Habilayn, a sandbagged tented Battalion base and air strip astride the road to Dhala, which Royal Marine Commandos handed over to the Battalion several times . . . and the oil drums had once more to be re-painted blue-red-blue! A company was based at Dhala, near the border with Yemen.

During the early stages of the Battalion's tour, No 3 Company was in a detached company base in the Wadi Matlah, some miles from the bulk of the Battalion at Habilayn. In the temporary absence of the company commander, the second-in-command, Capt David Webb-Carter, was in charge. That evening and with no warning a determined attack was pressed home on the company camp under heavy fire from small arms and blindicide rockets. (Blindicide means armour killer, as in Insecticide!) Capt Webb-Carter put up stout defence, and astonishingly the only casualty was the company's fridge, grievously wounded. It was reported that one of the Battalion's characters, L/Sgt 'The Bat' Tighe, a shortsighted, Arabic-speaking mortar fire controller, issued a stream of Irish Arabic fire orders to the confused opposition. Capt Webb-Carter was awarded the Military Cross.

Above: **Temple Hill Picquet, Dhala.** L/Cpls Jim Mooney and Stevenson and Gdsm Taylor.

Above: **L/Sgts Hoey and Noel Cullen** in a sangar up country with the unmistakable figure of Capt Shane Blewitt. In the foreground can be seen a wireless aerial of the fishing rod type.

Below: **Replen.** Eggs, water and rations being delivered to a picquet. Land Rovers were adapted to carry a General Purpose Machine Gun even for street patrols, while an angle Iron picquet was fitted to the front to counter the threat of piano wire stretched across the road.

Above: **Patrol near Habilayn.** Note the Commanding Officer, Lt-Col Tony Aylmer, nearest the camera, carries an Armalite rifle. He is followed by the Regimental Sergeant Major, Victor Sullivan.

Hearts and Minds patrols were undertaken in the mountains, and efforts were made to keep the wild Radfan countryside peaceful. Egyptian plastic anti-personnel mines were a worry up country, but seldom seen. There were numerous skirmishes and the Battalion set one hasty night ambush in which casualties were sustained from a volley of blindicides. Four died, amongst them the radio operator, so mortar fire could not be called down. L/Cpl Lewis won the Military Medal and Gdsm Bell was posthumously mentioned in dispatches.

History repeated itself when *The Harp*, a light-hearted Battalion newspaper was produced on a regular basis, echoing in style the levity and quality of its Great War trench predecessor, the *Morning Rire*.

During the Battalion's tour the 1967 Arab-Israeli war broke out. The locals, to a man, backed the Arabs with vigour and violence. There were taunting shouts from the urban rioters: 'Nasser Tamam', to which the Guardsmen boredly replied with the incomprehensible well worn Mick epithet 'Queen Victoria . . . very good bloke'! The situation became much inflamed by the mutiny of the Armed Police in Crater, an almost inaccessible inner suburb and trouble spot where The Northumberland Fusiliers suffered a number of casualties. Irish Guards companies were deployed to guard key points and patrolled the streets 24 hours a day. One night, communications with the platoon on duty at the oil refinery failed. Urgent investigation revealed a sporting

young officer improvising with the long aerial of the C42 wireless set, fishing for king fish.

During these operations, which spoiled the Commanding Officer's planned drinks party to celebrate the Queen's Birthday, No 3 Company was withdrawn and hurriedly flown (exhausted) to RAF Riyan near Mukalla. The same evening, in the Regiment's first live helicopter assault, part of a platoon secured the town of Sliyun up country in the Hadhramaut, followed shortly after by further deployment of the remainder of the company to Ghuraf air strip and Shibam, the Queen of Sheba's wonderful city in the wadi.

As time in Aden began to run out the local dockers went on strike and the Battalion found itself, in sizzling temperatures, loading valuable ammunition and stores which were to be evacuated by ships of the British India Line near Steamer Point.

Finally, the Barracks were handed over, less air conditioning, to the Russians!

History repeating itself. Not since the dock strike in 1949 had the Battalion loaded ships. This was another role as part of the Aden withdrawal.

Below left: **About to go on patrol in Sheik Othman.** L/Cpl 'Hovis' Brown *(left)* and L/Sgt Kelly closing the doors of a Bedford 3 Armoured 3 Ton Truck.

No 3 Company briefing before a Hearts and Minds operation. On left Sgt MacDermot and CSM Kelly.

On 1 June 1967 No 3 Company was attached to the Parachute Battalion; this was the day (The Glorious First of June) on which there were more than one hundred 'incidents' before midday. Incidents had become blurred by continual skirmishing and fighting in the streets, and to everyone's surprise the animals were released from the rather moth-eaten zoo. There was also the Federal National Guard (a swarthy bunch with an eye to the future!) and the Federal Regular Army who were more reliable and still had some brave British Officers. Most Beau Geste of all were the Hadrahmi Bedouin Legion who, whilst nominally helping No 3 Company at Siyun, were regarded with some suspicion since they had murdered their British Commanding Officer the previous week.

A Hadrahmi Bedouin Legionnaire.

L/Sgt 'The Bat' Tighe at Siyun, making the best use of his recently acquired Arabic in the hope of maintaining regular supplies.

An Aden policeman accompanied each foot patrol. A very smart police force operated under difficult circumstances.

Visit to Aden by the Colonel of the Regiment, 1967. Field Marshal Alex visited the Battalion and distributed the Shamrock. The Field Marshal commented that, with the exception of the helicopter, the tactics being used up country in Aden were the same as he had known when he commanded the Nowshera Brigade on the North West Frontier. Indeed, the Mountain Warfare pamphlet used for training was a re-write of the pre-war pamphlet of the same name.

The Field Marshal inspecting a newly introduced WOMBAT anti-tank gun. *L–R:* RSM Vic Sullivan; Major Peter Verney; the Field Marshal; Lt-Col Tony Aylmer, Commanding Officer; Capt John Lockwood, Adjutant. Just visible behind the commanding officer is the Trilby hat favoured by Assistant Regimental Adjutant Tony Mainwaring-Burton, always immaculately dressed even as a retired officer.

Officers of 1st Battalion Irish Guards, Aden, March 1967.
Back Row L–R: Major (QMS) Paddy Mercer MBE, MM; Capt Sean O'Dwyer; Lt Colijn Thomson-Moore; Capt David Moore (Medical Officer); Major Bob Kennedy; Capt Simon Gordon Duff (SG Air Platoon); Major Peter Verney; Father Michael Holman; Capt John Lockwood; Major Brian Gilbart-Denham; Major (Rtd) Tony Mainwaring-Burton; Capt Patrick Grayson; Lt Mickey Barnes (WG Air Platoon); The Rev Frank Johnson; Capt (QM) Arthur Bell; Capt David Webb-Carter MC; Capt Shane Blewitt.
Middle Row L–R: Major John Hallmark (Paymaster) Capt Paul de Remusat; Lt-Col Tony Aylmer (Commanding Officer); Field Marshal Alex; Major John Head; Capt Tom Brooke; Capt Christopher Wolverson.
Front Row L–R: 2/Lt David Carleton-Paget; 2/Lt Anthony Weldon; Lt Malcolm Ross (SG); Lt Savill Young; Lt Robin Bullock-Webster; 2/Lt Michael Chesterton.

The Battalion returned from Aden to Elizabeth Barracks, Pirbright. Here Queen Elizabeth The Queen Mother presented her Shamrock on St Patrick's Day 1968. This was followed, interspersed with Spearhead (the standby Battalion) and public duties, by the first EXERCISE POND JUMP WEST to Canada.

Boxing. The Regiment won the King's Trophy (the Army championship) in 1961, 1964 and 1966. Here the victorious 1966 team pose. Gdsm McKinty boxed for Ireland in the Olympic Games; the three O'Sullivan brothers (frequent 'visitors' to Commanding Officer's Orders) had a style all their own, and every man in the group was a character. The Regiment, following the tradition started by the first Quartermaster, Ginger Fowles, lived and breathed boxing and was intensely proud of these men. [Sadly Sergeant Fitzpatrick, back row extreme right, the trainer, was killed in Aden].

The Colonel in Chief, painted by Timothy Whidborne. The artist served in the Regiment between 1943 and 1948. This painting was presented to the Regiment by Capt Michael Boyle in 1969.

EXERCISE POND JUMP WEST, Canada, 1968.

Above: **In 1968 the Battalion was flown en masse to Canada for training on the Camp Wainwright Training Grounds in Alberta.** Also in attendance was Father Dolly Brookes from Downside who last served with the Regiment in the Second World War.

Above: **L/Sgt John Simpson** briefs his patrol before a trekking exercise.

Left: **The Quartermaster, Capt Arthur Bell,** entered into the spirit of things, although perhaps dressed for a few thousand miles to the south.

CYPRUS 1969

A Battalion exercise in Cyprus gave an opportunity for the Micks to meet the Irish Army which was providing a United Nations Battalion. Here the pipers from the Irish Army play together with those from 1st Battalion Irish Guards. L/Cpl Johnston late became Pipe Major.

A hurling match took place between the Irish Army Battalion and the Micks. Tactfully, the score was never recorded! *Left, nearest the camera:* L/Sgt Guerin. Also visible L/Cpl Fitzsimmonds. The Commanding Officer Lt-Col John Head MBE welcomes the teams.

Mini Miçks. In the late 1960s it was decided that a good means of stimulating the Irish Guards numbers enlisting as Junior Guardsmen or Junior Leaders would be to institute Cadet Platoons in Northern Ireland. Here Field Marshal Alex performs one of his last duties with the Regiment, visiting the Cadet Platoon in Belfast. *Left:* L/Sgt McNickle (in No2 Dress); the Colonel of the Regiment; CSM Bill Allister, the Regiment's recruiter in Belfast.

Funeral of Field Marshal the Earl Alexander of Tunis, Colonel of the Regiment, 24 June 1969. As a Knight of the Garter the Field Marshal's funeral service was in St George's Chapel at Windsor. Here, the gun carriage turns off the High Street up towards the Henry VIII Gate of the Castle. Sergeant Irwin leads the charger with the boots reversed, while three Irish Guards Field Officers carry cushions bearing the Field Marshal's decorations. The Regiment was saddened that he had not lived long enough to name the new Guards Depot barracks at Pirbright, which his widow duly named Alexander Barracks.

Shooting Team with trophies, 1970. Winners of the London District Rifle Association (LDRA). This was the era of great shooting teams. Not all the names were recorded, but almost thirty years later the following can be identified: *L–R Seated:* Sgt Shepherd; Sgt Chambers; D/Sgt Garner; Lt Philip O'Reilly; C/Sgt Roberts; Sgt Brown; L/Sgt Bittles. *Standing rows include:* Gdsm Byles and Lee; L/Sgt Leggatt; Gdsm Shanks; two Robinson brothers out of the four who eventually formed a strong family unit in the team, L/Cpl O'Neill and Furphy, as well as Gdsm Tobin at the top.

Recruit Mallet, tallest man in the Regiment, provided a challenge when he joined No 5 Company at the Guards Depot. Mallet, from Birmingham, stood 7ft 8 inches in a bearskin. Here Company Sergeant Major Tom Corcoran and L/Cpl Hanna from the tailor's shop pose for the photographer. Mallet was of course difficult to use for public duties, since he did not fit easily in a rank. However, he made a fine impression when opening the doors of visiting VIPs' cars.

HONG KONG 1970–1972

The Battalion flew to Hong Kong in late 1970. Battalion Headquarters and two companies were at Stanley Fort on the south side of Hong Kong Island while, because of refurbishment, the remainder of the Battalion was based at Lye Mun, some 25 minutes away on the north of the island.

The Battalion's role included border duties with the Royal Hong Kong Police, and support of the Civil Power as necessary. When carrying out tours of duty on the Chinese border, the Battalion came under command 48 Gurkha Infantry Brigade, based at Sek Kong in the New Territories. Their unpleasant task was to apprehend escapers, who had swum from China and who were seeking freedom in Hong Kong. They were viewed as illegal immigrants. The Police would question them, and then they were returned to China to an uncertain fate.

During the Battalion's tour in Hong Kong it experienced several spectacular typhoons (the first of which removed the paint from all the newly repainted Battalion signs). Another, Typhoon 'Rose' was said to have been the most severe for many years. Twelve ships were wrecked in Hong Kong Harbour.

Affectation? The Commanding Officer, Lt-Col Tony Plummer, borrowed the Adjutant's tactical brolly during EXERCISE HARD NUT and the photographer won the Army Photographer of the Year prize. The Adjutant, Capt Willie Mahon, just got drenched! 'It is,' the Duke of Wellington had said some time before, 'a needless affectation for officers of the Foot Guards to carry an umbrella upon the battlefield.' Major Savill Young was known to have done so at Anzio, so it is almost a regimental custom, despite the Iron Duke's exhortation.

Marching through Kowloon. Major Patrick Grayson leads No 2 Company down Nathan Road, Kowloon after the Queen's Birthday Parade, 21 April 1972. Keeping a supervisory eye from the roadside, D/Sgt Meredith. Their white No 3 Dress was known as Ice Cream Order. In Hong Kong the Queen's Birthday was celebrated on her actual birthday in April as it was too hot to do so on her Official Birthday in June.

Sixth Colonel of the Regiment. On the death of Field Marshal the Earl Alexander of Tunis, Lieutenant General Sir Basil Eugster was appointed Colonel. Here he is seen in Hong Kong in 1970 (he was Commander British Forces) with other Irish Guardsmen serving in, or as part of, No 1 (Guards) Independent Company, The Parachute Regiment, visiting the Colony. *Standing, L–R:* Sgt Armstrong (Orderly); Sgt Sinclair; CSM Kelly; RSM Micky Moran MM (Garrison Sergeant Major); the Colonel of the Regiment; Capt Colijn Thompson-Moore; Capt Patrick Grayson (ADC); D/Sgt Murphy; CSM Stewart. *Front Row, L–R:* Gdsm Hughes; Gdsm Passant; Gdsm Moss; Gdsm McGormick; Gdsm O'Connor; Gdsm Orrit; Gdsm Stevens.

Kotewall Road Disaster.
No 2 Company helping with search and rescue after freak monsoon rains had caused two high-rise residential buildings in a steep part of the Peak area to collapse in the middle of the night. Deep under the rubble, in a precarious cavity which was in danger of imminent collapse and which was filling with escaping gas, 2/Lt Johnny Gorman (son of John Gorman of King Tiger Tank, Normandy 1944) managed to undertake several hair-raising rescues for which he was awarded the George Medal. Gdsm Kennedy received the Queen's Commendation.

The George Medal.

8 Irish Guards held, then freed by PLA

By KEVIN SINCLAIR

CHINESE troops applauded and cheered early today as they escorted eight Irish soldiers back to the Hongkong border.

Earlier, the Chinese hosted the British soldiers at a fish and crab dinner on the other side of the wire at the divided border village of Shataukok.

The Famous Border Incident. The Battalion set off for yet another border tour on 18 May 1971. The easternmost company base was Shataukok, in which No2 Company deployed. CQMS 'Joe' Skates, fully aware of the importance of not straying across the border, was in the lead Land Rover, delivering supplies and stragglers to the company outlying positions. He turned round to ensure that the 3 tonner was following, only to find that his driver had crossed the border. Frantically trying to reverse, he now found his way blocked by the 3 tonner. They were instantly apprehended by the People's Liberation Army. At once the

incident hit the world's headlines. The untold truth was that the Battalion thought it knew who was in the convoy. However, the Chinese announced they held eight, not seven, British soldiers. Unbeknown to all, one Guardsman had been late for the main convoy to the border that morning. To avoid being reported absent, he quietly 'stowed away' in the back of the CQMS's truck, the last to leave Stanley. His plan was working well until the navigation problem, when instead of quietly taking up his position in his platoon, he ended up in China. Imagine the confusion!

The border "incident" began at 2.15 pm yesterday when a group of Irish Guards soldiers drove towards British Army positions near the China border – and kept on driving.

They ended up well inside Chinese territory.

The truck and landrover in the convoy were both carrying provisions for British troops.

When the Quarter Master Sergeant J. Skates realised he was in Chinese territory, the two vehicles stopped.

A Hongkong policeman, who reacted much faster than the soldiers, quickly grabbed an electronic microphone and yelled: "You are in Chinese territory. Don't move."

Curious Chinese troops

The troops stayed in their trucks. Peoples Liberation Army men quickly surrounded them, more curious than dangerous.

Then, under PLA foot guard, the two vehicles moved around the corner and out of view of the anxious Hongkong police watchers.

Early today, it was found the troops were ordered out of the trucks by Chinese troops soon after they were out of the sight of our border watchers.

Then they went into a police station where their identities were checked.

Finally, the Chinese troops asked the Irishmen to go to a dinner party, where fish, crabs and prawns were served.

The personnel involved in the incident were: C.Q.M.S. J. Skates, L/Cpl. K. Gillen, Guardsmen B. Donnelly, N. Egan, C. Lavery, C. McMenamin, T. Meyler, A. Cullen.

The Regimental Band, visiting the Battalion in Belize, out of tunics!

1972-3

The Battalion returned from Hong Kong to Caterham in late 1972. While it was in Hong Kong the Army introduced the new Disruptive Pattern Material combat dress (initially christened 'Flower Power'), in place of the former plain green combat dress. After Hong Kong there followed a short tour, under Lt-Col Giles Allan, to Belize. This was the Battalion's first of many visits to the former British Honduras, countering external threats to the former colony.

Above: **Escort to the Colour,** June 1973. Subaltern, Capt Barry Gubbins, Ensign 2/Lt Jonathan Coe, Regimental Sergeant Major Frank Groves (the only Regimental Sergeant Major to have been Pipe Major). In the background is the Guards Memorial, a subscription to which was made by Rudyard Kipling, in memory of his son, John, from the proceeds of the sale of the regimental history, *The Irish Guards in the Great War.*

Right: **Major-General's Inspection, Caterham 1974 – Second Orders.** During Major-General Philip Ward's inspection Sgt Tony Kirk, No 1 Company encourages innovative PT.

In 1975 the Battalion moved to Bulle Barracks, Munster to be part of the 4th Guards Brigade.

Germany, 1976. Lt-Col Dick Hume, the Commanding Officer, debriefs No 1 Company during an exercise on the Haltern training area.

Chieftain tanks supporting the Irish Guards Battle Group on training at Sennelager.

Army Inter-Unit Cookery Champions, 1976 (previously won in 1913!). One means of keeping morale high was the Commanding Officer's insistence on good food. The Regimental Cooks, for the last time, since they were rebadging to the Army Catering Corps, under Sgt Clavin, won the 2nd Armoured Division, BAOR and Army championships. As the Regimental *Journal* reported with delight: 'The competition required them to set up a field kitchen properly camouflaged, and for two of them to cook a three course meal for twenty men on a Number One burner, while the rest did the same in the kitchen . . . Nobody knew until the day who would be selected to cook what.' The menus never varied, much to the regret of certain inhabitants of the Guardroom who were required to eat fish liberally covered in white sauce every day for three months. But as the Messing Officer so kindly put it: 'Some actually grew to like it.'

Belize, 1977. Summer 1977 was sunny and Silver Jubilee Year, and 1st Battalion Irish Guards was at Munster. The day after the Queen's Jubilee Review at Sennelager, No 2 Company under Major Sean O'Dwyer was flown on a six-month emergency tour to Belize, where mounting security problems necessitated reinforcement.

HMS *Boxer,* a Type 42 guided missile destroyer. Throughout its history, the Regiment has enjoyed close ties with the Royal Navy. *Boxer* became the affiliated ship in 1984. She was decommissioned on 4 August 1999. Numerous groups from the Regiment visited the ship, and the strong friendship and admiration for the Royal Navy flourished.

OPERATION BURBERRY. In late 1977 the Fire Brigades Union called a nation-wide strike over pay. The Armed Services were equipped with venerable Green Goddess fire appliances, originally designed for the Auxiliary Fire Service, and which had been in store since the 1950s. All Regimental Headquarters deployed to sectors of London. The Irish Guards, under Colonel Giles Allan, went to Hounslow and controlled the South-West sector of London. 1st Battalion Irish Guards took its place in the roster during the strike, and so did recruits from the Guards Depot. Several daring rescues were made. The greatest difficulty was preventing Guardsmen with no breathing apparatus or protective clothing risking their own lives for others. Here L/Sgt D. McDonnell rescues a child from a burning building. (Courtesy *Daily Mail*)

Firefighting. Recruits from the Guards Depot deployed on OPERATION BURBERRY.

The Robinson Brothers. Just as there were O'Sullivan Brothers in the boxing team, so the family factor was evident in the shooting team. All four Robinson brothers were members of the Household Division shooting team. Three brothers shot for the Army, and three brothers shot for Ireland. This is the only time in Bisley's history that four brothers shot for the same regiment at the same time. *L–R:* John, David, Kenneth and Stephen. They are pictured standing on the Green in front of the Officers' Mess at Victoria Barracks, Windsor.

New Colours, Windsor, 1978. The Colonel in Chief presented new Colours on the East Terrace at Windsor. Lt-Col James Baker, Commanding Officer, accompanies Her Majesty during the inspection. In her speech The Queen referred to the Colours of the disbanded Irish Regiments which are in safekeeping in Windsor Castle.

Laying up the Old Colours, Windsor, 1978. These Colours, presented by The Queen in 1966, were laid up at the Garrison Church, Windsor in October 1978. Here the Colonel of the Regiment takes the Colours from Colonel Giles Allan (Regimental Lieutenant Colonel) and Lt-Col James Baker, Commanding Officer.

Drum Sergeant Kirkland, Army motor cycle champion, 1978.

Overseas Training in Ghana, July 1978. Major Robin Bullock-Webster took No 4 Company to Ghana, where Piper Stranix proved an instant attraction.

ST PATRICK'S DAY 1980

Clement Weather? This is one of those famous occasions which nobody who was there will ever forget. It rained, the forecast said it would lift, but it just got worse. The Battalion, about to enter the public duties season after Belize, was wearing tunics for the first time, and The Queen and The Queen Mother were attending. Miraculously the tunics survived. However, the guests' canvas chairs filled with water when they stood for the National Anthem . . . so there was a curious reluctance to sit down.

Two smiling Queens on St Patrick's Day, the weather notwithstanding.

Rhodesia, 1980. The Commonwealth Monitoring Force was assembled in Rhodesia to enable the 'Freedom Fighters' to hand in their weapons and to allow free elections to take place. Major Tim Purdon, and Sergeant Jimmy Hagan are seen here discussing matters with new arrivals. Their Assembly Area, FOXTROT, eventually housed several thousand Communist trained ZANU and ZAPU freedom fighters who retained their weapons until the last moment. Football was one magic ingredient in keeping all happy. So was the fact that the Africans were pleased to be hosted by soldiers whom they mistakenly supposed to be Irish freedom fighters! Nobody discussed politics, and they were never disabused. A special medal was struck for this unusual operation. Major Tim Purdon was awarded the MBE for his work at Assembly Area FOXTROT.

The Rhodesia Medal.

Irish Guards Monitors in Rhodesia, 1980. *L–R:* Capt The Hon Jeremy Stopford; Sgt L. Templeton with pipes; Sgt J Knowles; Sgt B McMahon; Sgt A. McCrum; L/Sgt Don Kearney – who has contributed greatly to this book – L/Sgt A. Mahon; L/Sgt L. Liddy; Sgt D. Cullen; L/Sgt J. Fitzpatrick; Capt Sebastian Roberts; Major Tim Purdon; L/Sgt M. Doherty; Sgt T. McGran.

Army Athletics Champions, 1981. Between 1980 and 1984 the Battalion athletics team were Army Champions twice, and runners up to 50 Missile Regiment, Royal Artillery on three occasions. For five years they were in the finals of the competition.

Not shown: Sgt Templeton; Sgt Rimmer; L/Sgt Leyland; L/Cpl Benn; Gdsm Hughes; Gdsm Foley; Gdsm McKay; Gdsm Brotherston.
Back row, L–R: L/Sgt Collister; Gdsm McCallion; L/Cpl Farrell; L/Cpl Frazer; Gdsm Redmonds; Gdsm Dunn; L/Sgt Railton; Pte Kay, ACC.
Centre row, L–R: L/Sgt Horrigan; Gdsm Steed; Gdsm Walsh; Gdsm Bailey; L/Cpl Meadows; Gdsm Gregg; L/Cpl Grundie; Gdsm Gavin; L/Sgt Hemphill; L/Cpl Dunn; Gdsm Roach.
Front row, L–R: Cpl Shields, ACC; L/Sgt Veness; Major J.B. O'Gorman; C/Sgt Mooney; Lt–Col D.B.W. Webb-Carter MC; CSM Lowe; RSM McLean; Sgt Welsh; L/Sgt Dawson
Trophies: Prince of Wales Relay Cup; Eastern Area Cup; Lawson Cup; Major Unit Challenge Shield; Field Events Cup; Carrington Cup; Sir Maurice Deane Trophy; London District Cup.

Chelsea Bus Bomb, 10 October 1981. The dismounting Tower Guard was approaching Chelsea Barracks when an IRA nail bomb made with heavy coach bolts was exploded at close range to their bus. Twenty-three NCOs and Guardsmen were injured. The following day Prime Minister, Margaret Thatcher, inspected the bus and then visited the injured in hospital. She is seen here talking to Gdsm Jones. Sgt Cullen and Gdsm Trafford were each awarded the British Empire Medal for their work on that occasion, the latter for performing a life saving improvised tracheotomy on a casualty on the pavement. In a truly touching gesture, a Dutch family living in Nijmegen who rememberd the 3rd Battalion in the war, sent a letter of sympathy, saying *'you did so much for us, now let us do some small thing for you',* and included a donation for the welfare of the casualties.

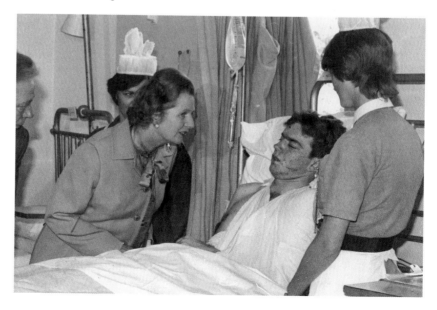

Training on the Dorbaum training area, Münster, 1983. The APCs pictured have a commander's turret with a pintle mounted GPMG. L/Cpl Morgan, the company piper, plays the heroic role.

Brigade Commander's Visit to Oxford Barracks, Münster, 1982. Brigadier Charles Guthrie, late Welsh Guards, Commander 4th Armoured Brigade (later Chief of Defence Staff) visits No 4 Company. *L–R:* RSM V. McLean, Capt Patrick Johns, Major Henry Wilson. *Partly obscured:* Lt-Col Robert Corbett, Lt Gavin Robinson, CSM 'Hovis' Brown, Capt David Hurley (The Royal Australian Regiment),Brigadier Charles Guthrie, Major Brian O'Gorman, OC 4 Coy.

Sennelager, May 1984. Sennelager, a huge training area in Germany originally used by the Wehrmacht, became in the 1960s one of NATO's finest range complexes, under British Army management. It remains a key live training area. Here GPMG teams from No 4 Company are field firing. *L–R:* Sgt Collister, Gdsm McMullen, Woods and Swift.

Statue of Field Marshal The Earl Alexander of Tunis. On 8 May 1985 The Queen unveiled a statue of Field Marshal Alex outside the Guards Chapel. This was one of the new Colonel, HRH The Grand Duke's first public appearances in London. *L–R:* L/Cpl J. Mateer; in morning coat The 2nd Earl Alexander of Tunis, HRH the Colonel, HM The Queen (almost invisible) and Lt Col Sean O'Dwyer, Commanding Officer 1st Battalion Irish Guards.

The sixth Colonel of the Regiment, General Sir Basil Eugster KCVO, KCB, CBE, DSO, MC, died on 5 April 1984. At the request of the Regiment, Her Majesty the Queen invited HRH The Grand Duke of Luxembourg KG, who had served as a young officer in 3rd Battalion Irish Guards during the Second World War, to take on the role. He was appointed on 21 August 1984. Colonel John, as he became known at once, endeared himself to everybody by stating in the Messroom during a visit to the Battalion that he was thrilled by the appointment, and breaking into that familiar barrack room intonation used when stating your kit for an inspection, the new colonel ringingly announced that he was here 'at the service of the Regiment'. The Messroom roof nearly lifted with the cheering.

The Field Marshal's cap decorated for St Patrick's Day, 1998. This photograph may be out of sequence, but it is placed here to illustrate something indefinable about the Mick character. Somehow, the Regiment likes to convince itself that this sort of gesture of affectionate irreverence would never 'rub' in some of our more stately sister regiments!

Academy Sergeant Major Dennis Cleary at the Royal Military Academy Sandhurst. This is the senior warrant officer's appointment in the Army and the first time held by an Irish Guardsman.

Role Playing at the ARU, Newcastle Barracks, Hamm, 18 April 1985. The Annual Review of a Unit, unlike the old Major General's Inspections, was changed to involve a serious tactical element, coupled with a rigorous administrative 'dig out'. A captured senior 'enemy officer', Capt Sebastian Roberts, is being questioned by the acting commanding officer, Major Brian Holt, while CQMS T. Lee keeps a smart watch on proceedings. All this is under observation by Divisional Staff, including a future Inspector of Prisons, General David Ramsbotham.

Alwyn Charlton reads the Citation for the Victoria Cross won by his brother, Eddie, a matter of paces from the scene of the action. (For full citation see p. 210)

Winners of the Langton Trophy, 1985, The Corps of Drums. Drum Major 'Dixie' Dean MEM receives the trophy watched by the Commanding Officer, Lt-Col Robert Corbett at Woodlands Camp, Sennelager.

The Langton Trophy. The Langton Trophy is an annual inter-platoon competition started in 1964 by the Commanding Officer, Lt-Col Stephen Langton MVO, MC. The trophy itself is a representation of the Armoured Humber 1 Ton APC (known not very affectionately as the 'Pig') with which the Battalion manouevred round Germany (in the 1960s).

Pristina, 13 June 1999. After months of terror, the surviving ethnic Albanians slowly emerge to greet Four Company, Irish Guards. It was more than an hour before the Albanians felt safe enough to gather on the streets. The atmosphere was still extremely volatile – even as the up-armoured Warriors drove in, defiant Serbs streamed past them, firing wildly.

CHAPTER SEVEN

1986–2000

END OF
THE CENTURY

This period saw the role of the Army changing rapidly from its Cold War concentration on the defence of West Germany, to a smaller force that was increasingly deployed worldwide, on peace support operations. The Battalion started and ended this era based in Münster, Westfalia. In 1986 it was a mechanised Battalion, part of the 1st British Corps, but by 1999 it was an armoured Battalion, part of the one British division remaining on the European mainland for deployment worldwide.

During these hectic years the Irish Guards had six main moves. They were in Berlin in 1990 when the Wall came down. There were operational tours, twice to Northern Ireland, to Belize and to the Balkans. Companies also deployed operationally to the Falkland Islands, to Northern Ireland, and to Hong Kong just before the handover to China. Detachments were sent to help the affiliated The Royal Montserrat Defence Force cope with the effects of volcanic eruptions. There were training exercises in Kenya, Oman, Denmark, Canada and Cyprus.

When in England the Battalion played its full part in public duties and new Colours were presented and trooped twice.

The major operational feature of this period was the Battalion's role in the relief of Kosovo in 1999.

Major General's Inspection, Chelsea Barracks, 1986. Major-General Christopher Airey inspects the Corps of Drums and The Pipes accompanied by the Adjutant, Major Bernard Hornung. In the background can be seen the Commander Supply, London District, the only Lieutenant Colonel's Post in the then Royal Army Ordnance Corps still to be entitled to wear a frock coat.

The Queen's Birthday at Windsor. The Windsor Castle Guard, augmented for The Queen's Birthday, commanded by Major Brian Holt, 21 April 1986. Here Her Majesty passes the Guard on return from St George's Chapel.

EXERCISE BRITANNIA WAY/IBERIAN FOCUS, 1986. In 1986 an exchange exercise took place with the Spanish Army. A platoon from the Spanish Infantry Regiment of Mallorca, No 13, based at Lorca, Murcia, came to England, and No 1 Company went to Lorca. Here L/Cpl Hughes instructs Spanish conscript soldiers on the 9mm Sterling Sub Machine Gun.

EXERCISE POND JUMP WEST, Canada, 1987. Lt-Col Henry Wilson, the Commanding Officer, with Pipe Major Fraser and the Pipes. Note the new helmet worn by the Commanding Officer made of a new composite material, lighter and stronger than steel.

The Old and Bold. Marching past Her Majesty on St Patrick's Day, 1987. In this photograph some distinguished veterans are visible. Leading is Brigadier Michael Gordon-Watson, who won his first MC in Palestine, his second in Norway and his third at Anzio. Next to him is Major Sir Oliver Chesterton MC, who won his in 1943 for capturing the Bou feature. Next to him is Brigadier Mick O'Cock who won his MC commanding a squadron of 2nd Battalion in Normandy in 1944. Colonel Tony Aylmer who served in the 3rd Battalion and commanded the 1st Battalion in Aden follows him, followed in turn by Brigadier Savill Young DSO who was decorated for Anzio. Also featured on Parade is Major Hugh Ripman RAMC whose redoubtable efforts with Mick casualties in 1944/45 have forever endeared him to the Regiment.

Preparations for a charity abseil from the roof of the highest hotel in Europe, the Forum in Brompton Road, London, 8 November 1987. *L–R:* Capt James Stopford; Sgt Cardy and Capt Colin Butterworth.

Tunisia Battlefield Tour, 1987. A group of some sixty members of the Regiment and their wives visited Tunisia to follow the 1943 actions of the 1st Battalion. Here the veterans pose in the area of the Doll's House (Battalion Headquarters near Medjez el Bab). *L–R:* Major Sir Oliver Chesterton MC; Lt-Col Jack Pestell MBE; Major Owen McInerney (from Canada); Major Brian Synge; Ex L/Cpl John Kenneally VC; Ex Gdsm Bill Crawford (from Australia); Ex Sgt Jim Ryan MM; Lt-Col Jimmy Kelly OBE; Ex Gdsm John Cooney (one of two Irish Guards survivors from Recce Ridge); Ex Company Sergeant Major Gerry Whelan; Capt Mungo Park MBE; Major Colin Kennard DSO; Major Charles Larking; Major Mike Rawlence; Ex Gdsm Richardson; and Major-General Drew Bethell (the Royal Artillery officer from Recce Ridge). The Colonel of the Regiment, HRH The Grand Duke of Luxembourg, attended semi-incognito under the guise of Colonel Connor. (Connor was the name of the wolfhound at the time.) All was fine until one day the coach grounded. The Arab driver, nicknamed Seamus, turned to the Colonel who was sitting in front, and with Arab-American informality said 'You'll have to push, Dook!' And he did.

Queen's Birthday Parade, 1988. This was the first Birthday Parade with the new SA80 rifle. There were still eight guards on parade (later reduced to six, so only one 'round the corner'). The Queen travelled by open carriage to the parade for the second year, Burmese, her fine Canadian mount having retired after the 1986 Birthday Parade. The Ensign was 2/Lt Stephen Segrave, and the Regimental Sergeant Major Vince McEllin.

Laying up of Colours, Guards Chapel, 5 September 1988.

Normandy Battlefield Tour, 1988. Ex Guardsman Dick Russell, a stretcher-bearer speaks about the 3rd Battalion at Sourdeval, watched by Colonel William Harvey-Kelly, a platoon commander at the time. There were many who wanted to return to Normandy to hear from those who had been there what had happened to the 2nd and 3rd Battalions in 1944. So a tour was arranged, which included a representative of X Company Scots Guards. Seeing and hearing the veterans talk, and hearing their moving stories was a wonderful experience. Much of what they said was noted and a full photographic record placed in the Regimental Archives. Perhaps an unexpectedly vivid lesson to come from it was that the characters of the regiment in 1944 were so similar to those of 1988. Wit and wickedness, fun and fear, somehow that old spirit spanned the generations, unchanged by the passing of time.

Jungle exercise in Belize. The Battalion operated in the Northern Battle Group area for the 1988 exercises.

Regimental Band visits Paris and the Arc de Triomphe, June 1989. Sadly, this was the last appearance with the Band of the Director of Music, Lt-Col Mick Lane.

The Battalion took its turn in the continuing defence of Belize against external threat.

Distribution of Shamrock, Belize, 1989. The Colonel of the Regiment visited Belize and distributed Queen Elizabeth's gift of Shamrock. The dress is light weight combat dress, and officers' berets now carry an embroidered bullion star taken from the Mess jacket (hence without the date 1783 which signifies the year of foundation of The Order Of St Patrick). *L–R:* The Commanding Officer, Lt-Col Brian Holt; RQMS Knowles; The Colonel, HRH The Grand Duke of Luxembourg; The Quartermaster, Major Bill Matthews MBE; Capt Hugh Howard-Allen.

Belize, March 1989. A Scimitar recce vehicle, mounting the Rarden 30mm cannon follows the marching party.

Training in Belize.

The 1st Battalion found itself stationed in Berlin at the epic moment when the Wall was dismantled, and Germany had yet to be re-united. Owing to reorganisation within the Foot Guards, the Regimental Lieutenant Colonel's role became open to senior officers. In 1989 Major General Robert Corbett, the Regimental Lieutenant Colonel, was posted to Berlin, as was the Battalion. He can be seen in the photograph wearing the Foot Guards pattern frock coat (in the rank of Colonel) which would not have been appropriate under any other circumstances for the GOC Berlin.

A Special Pipe Banner. HM Queen Elizabeth The Queen Mother's long and close friendship with the Regiment was marked in a personal way on St Patrick's Day in Berlin in 1990 when she presented her personal pipe banner, bearing her coat of arms, to be used by the Pipe Major. This is the only pipe banner in the Regiment and bears a star of St Patrick on the reverse. Pipe Major Kevin Fraser was the first Irish Guards Piper to become the Senior Pipe Major in the Household Division.

Shillelagh: the Battalion's Ceiledh band looking for an audience at the Brandenburg Gate, Berlin. *L–R:* RSM Knowles; Stephanie Shields; CQMS Shields; L/Cpl Trainor; D/Sgt Lavery and L/Sgt McCarthy.

Gdsm 'Big Red' McCloskey talking to Major-General Robert Corbett during his farewell visit to the Battalion, Berlin, October 1990.

Milan firing. The Milan anti-tank missile system replaced the 120mm recoilless SS guns of the BAT series.

Feu de Joie. No 2 Company, commanded by Major Bernard Hornung, fires a *feu de joie* during The Queen's Birthday Parade in the Olympic Stadium Berlin, 1990.

Irish Guards Football Team, winners of the Infantry Cup, 1991. *Back:* L/Sgt Leinster; L/Cpl Fagin; Gdsm Dillon; L/Cpl Withers; Gdsm Campbell; D/Sgt Cloney; Gdsm Mooney; L/Sgt Parkins; C/Sgt Wynne; Lt-Col Christopher Langton; RSM Knowles. *Front Row:* L/Sgt Davies; L/Cpl Doyle; L/Sgt McComb; Capt Robbie Kelly; Sgt Halliday; L/Sgt Halliday; L/Sgt Donaldson; L/Sgt Brennan; Capt Venning.

The London Branch of the Regimental Association on St Patrick's Day, 1991, at the Guards Depot, Pirbright. Major Tony Mainwaring-Burton, Chairman of the London Branch, and members give three cheers for Her Majesty Queen Elizabeth the Queen Mother.

Leaving for Schleswig-Holstein. Members of No 1 Company, Capt James Campbell-Johnston, L/Sgt Burge and L/Sgt Leinster, preparing to leave Berlin by cattle truck to go training in Schleswig-Holstein, September 1991.

Connor's Last Parade. Connor, heading for retirement, leads the Band away on St Patrick's Day, 1992 at Wavell Barracks, Berlin. Connor's successor was Malachy.

With the fall of the Berlin Wall visits were exchanged between the Allies (British, Americans and French) and the Soviet Forces. Here Pipe Major Stranix explains the Irish secret weapon to the Russians.

Training in Berlin.
House clearing skills being practised at Rhuleben Fighting City. A grenade having just been thrown through the window, the entrymen follow.

EXERCISE MEDICINE MAN, Alberta, Canada. Lt Taylor's Platoon Headquarters resting from the heat and dust.

Another Mick, another camel. Capt David Hannah on duty as a MINURSO United Nations observer in the disputed Sahara territory claimed by both the Polisario guerrillas and the Moroccans.

Operational Tour in Northern Ireland, OPERATION BANNER: November 1992-May 1993. The Battalion undertook its first operational tour in Fermanagh. In the picture Malachy is seen with members of No 2 Company at Derenish Island. *(Photo courtesy of Soldier Magazine).*

Tango 30 Alfa. No 6 Platoon, 2 (Operations)Company on the helipad at St Angelo security force base in Fermanagh, before deploying to patrol the Beleek Triangle. *Back row L–R:* Gdsm Dillon; Gdsm Cartwright; Gdsm Dawes; Gdsm Doyle 36; Lance Corporal Ruddock; L/Sgt Taylor; Gdsm Holmes; L/Cpl Martin. *Front Row L–R:* Gdsm Wyse; Gdsm Woodham; 2/Lt Lloyd Thomas; Gdsm Irwin; Gdsm Preuss.

Winter in Fermanagh. Patrolling continued in all weathers. This 'multiple' is heading off in snow, but the abiding memory of winter 1993 is of rain, rain, and yet more rain.

Grosvenor Barracks, Enniskillen, St Patrick's Day, 1993. Major General Robert Corbett, by now the Major General Commanding the Household Division, watches the march past. He is flanked by Drummer Coates with Malachy, and by L/Sgt Tumelty.

Malachy and Drummer Coates. Malachy died suddenly in October 1993 following a visit to the dentist. A magnificent and much loved mascot, he is buried in Chelsea Barracks. (*Photo* Mike Hollist)

The Colonel's Dinner, State Apartments, The Royal Hospital Chelsea, 10 September 1993. The Colonel of the Regiment was entertained to dinner by the Regimental Lieutenant Colonel Brigadier David Webb-Carter OBE, MC and his predecessors after the Colonel's portrait by Theodore Ramos had been unveiled. *Front Row, L–R:* Brigadier M.J.P. O'Cock CBE, MC; Colonel P.F.I. Reid OBE; Brigadier D.H. FitzGerald DSO; The Colonel of the Regiment HRH The Grand Duke of Luxembourg; Brigadier D.M.L. Gordon-Watson OBE, MC**; Brigadier H.L.S. Young DSO; Colonel C.W.D. Harvey-Kelly. *Back Row L–R:* Colonel Sir William Mahon Bt; Brigadier J.N. Ghika CBE; Colonel J.A. Aylmer; Colonel G.A. Allan OBE; Brigadier R.T.P. Hume; Brigadier D.B.W. Webb-Carter OBE, MC.

50th Anniversary of the Liberation of Luxembourg.
The Regimental Lieutenant Colonel, the Commanding Officer, Lt-Col Sebastian Roberts, the Regimental Band, the Pipes and No 1 Company travelled to Luxembourg for the celebrations. They were kindly entertained at Château Colmar Berg by the Colonel of the Regiment and the Grand Duchess.

RSM Brennan and Cuchulain comparing moustaches.

St Patrick's Day, 1995, Chelsea Barracks. Always the same, yet always different and for ever special. Her Majesty The Queen with Queen Elizabeth The Queen Mother and the Colonel (who had just been appointed a General) as the Regiment gives three cheers for the Queen Mother. This was the first parade for the new young wolfhound, Cuchulain.

Arnhem Cemetery. Commemoration of the 50th Anniversary of OPERATION MARKET GARDEN 1944 in which the Regiment played such a prominent part. Veterans from all Regiments returned to Holland and attended ceremonies in their honour.

VE Day 50th Anniversary Parade and service at Newtownards Co. Down, 1995. The Regimental Band in Conway Square. The Irish Guards Association members are on the front right of the parade.

A Family Regiment, 6 February 1996. The Roberts Family is inspected by their mother on mounting Queen's Guard. At the end of his time in command Lt-Col Sebastian Roberts *(right)* mounted Queen's Guard as Captain, with his brother Major Cassian Roberts *(left)* as the Subaltern, and his younger brother, Fabian *(centre)* as the Ensign.

OPERATION BANNER, East Tyrone, June-December 1995. Members of No 1 Company move forward to be deployed by Chinook helicopter from Dungannon, East Tyrone.

The annual Mick training team to Montserrat led by Major T. MacMullen changed roles at short notice to help with a non-combatant evacuation operation (NEO), OPERATION HARLECH, when volcanic activity in the Soufriere Hills started to erupt in July 1995.

Left: **The Irish Guards Training Team** with the gently steaming volcano in the background.
L–R: Lt John Skerrit MDF; Major John Lynch OC MDF; Sgt Buckley; Lt Rupert Lockwood.

The MDF being briefed in the presence of the Mick team on the left and the Royal Marines on the right at the main cricket ground, Plymouth. The Lynx is from HMS *Southampton*, the West Indies Guard Ship, whose Captain was commanding the NEO.

Above: **Sgt McCarthy supervising the offloading of stores from an RAF Hercules** at Montserrat International Airport, 25 August.

Above: **The tented city for evacuees** in the north of the island at Gerald's Bottom.

Left and Right: **The first large eruption** of the volcano on 20 August.

East Tyrone, 1995. L/Cpl McCool and Gdsm Finegan on patrol.

President of Ireland's Inspection, June 1996. The President, Mrs Mary Robinson, visited The Queen at Buckingham Palace. A Guard of Honour, found by No 1 Company commanded by Major James Stopford, Subaltern; Capt Christopher Ghika; Ensign, Lt Fabian Roberts, was inspected.

Mini Micks. Irish Guards Cadet detachments took part in a competition arranged by No 2 Company during a recruiting tour of Northern Ireland. The winners were the Liverpool Detachment who are seen with the trophy they have just received from the Commanding Officer Lt-Col James Pollock.

Normandy Battlefield Tour, July 1996. Capt Vivian Taylor arranged a tour to Normandy, Belgium and Holland where the 2nd and 3rd Battalions had fought. Twenty-five veterans were accompanied by serving members of the 1st Battalion. In Cagny they were fêted by the Mayor and French veterans.

Oman. EXERCISE ROCKY LANCE I. Lt J.F. Webb inspecting the food … goat … during No 2 Company's joint training with the Omani Army at Sur, March 1996.

EXERCISE ROCKY LANCE II. L/Sgt Clarke and L/Cpl Woodham apparently enjoying a meal of mutton during the exercise in the Wahiba Sands, September 1996.

Oman, September 1996. No 4 Company. The deployment which lasted for a month followed No 2 Company's similar exercise in March the same year.

Falkland Islands, October 1996–March 1997. No 1 Company provided the Falkland Islands Reinforced Infantry Company. L/Sgt Nicholson leads his patrol off from an outlying settlement.

Patrol in the Falklands,
1997. A No 1 Company patrol with locals. (*Photo* PA News).

Kenya. EXERCISE MONOPRIX, April 1997. No 2 Company commanded by Major James Patrick spent a month training in Kenya near Nanyuki. Lt Cahal O'Reilly, Sgt Moffett and L/Sgt Martin decide the best course of action as 5 Platoon prepares to attack.

Kenya. EXERCISE MONOPRIX, April 1997. 5 Platoon training at Impala Farm.

New Colours, Windsor, 22 May 1997. The Battalion commanded by Lt Colonel James Pollock MBE, formed up in the Quadrangle prior to the presentation of Colours by Her Majesty The Queen.

Presentation of Colours, May 1997. The Queen addresses the Battalion.

The Field Of Remembrance, November 1997. The Chairman of the London Branch of the Irish Guards Association, Colonel Giles Allan, at the Regimental Plot, with Association Members attending the annual ceremony of dedication and remembrance at Westminster Abbey.

Left: **St Patrick's Day Celebrations,** London, 15 March 1998. With the Battalion abroad once again in Münster, and no Guards Depot any longer at Pirbright to host St Patrick's Day, the Annual March to the Guards Memorial, which is now celebrated on the Sunday nearest St Patrick's Day, was combined with the distribution of Shamrock at Wellington Barracks. Queen Elizabeth's gift of Shamrock was distributed by Mr John Kenneally VC. *L–R:* RQMS D. Ryan; Mr John Kenneally VC; Brigadier Christopher Wolverson OBE, Regimental Lieutenant Colonel; Major Mick Henderson, Director of Music; Colonel Giles Allan OBE, Chairman London Branch Irish Guards Association; Capt Edward Boanas. In Germany the Grand Duchess distributed the Shamrock on behalf of The Queen Mother.

Right: **Warriors in Germany,** February 1998. The Battalion converted to the Armoured Infantry role, equipped with Warrior Armoured Infantry Fighting Vehicles. The local training area for much of the initial manoeuvring was at Haltern. During 1998 the Battalion was constantly training, including undertaking simulated Virtual Reality Armoured Training with the United States Army at Grafenwohr and deploying to Canada for EXERCISE MEDICINE MAN.

Right: **The Island of Ireland Peace Park at Messines** commemorates all those who fought and died in the First World War. It was unveiled by The Queen and the President of Ireland, in the presence of King Albert of the Belgians, 11 November 1998.

Above: **Warriors of Nos 1 and 4 Companies advance to contact during company training at Haltern.**

Left: **12 Platoon 4 Coy tactics at Haltern.**

KOSOVO

In early 1999 the 1st Battalion Irish Guards was stationed in Münster, having just completed a year of conversion to the Armoured Infantry role in Warrior Armoured Fighting Vehicles.

The Kosovo crisis arose suddenly and in February No 1 Company deployed to Macedonia as part of the King's Royal Hussars Battle Group. It was intended that this should form part of a monitoring force. Meanwhile the rest of the battalion formed the backbone of a separate Irish Guards Battle Group. This consisted of Battalion Headquarters, Numbers 4 and Support Company 1st Battalion Irish Guards, A (King Harald's) Company 1st Battalion Green Howards, D Squadron King's Royal Hussars, 52 Battery Royal Artillery and 26 Armoured Engineer Squadron. The Irish Guards Battle Group waited at three days notice to move before deploying to Macedonia in late April

After a long bombing campaign by NATO, both the King's Royal Hussars and the Irish Guards Battle Groups entered Kosovo on 12 June. The Irish Guards were the first NATO troops to reach the capital, Pristina, where they were rapturously welcomed despite the real threats from the Serbian Army. Order was restored as the Serb Army withdrew

St Patrick's Day, Prilep, Macedonia, 1999. Major Michael Moriarty and No 1 Company Group give the customary three cheers for Her Majesty Queen Elizabeth The Queen Mother.

The main body of the Irish Guards Battle Group was augmented by A Company of the Green Howards, providing a makeshift shower for C/Sgt Bennett, Milan Platoon, second in command.

Pre K-Day Training.
Members of 1 Company serving with the King's Royal Hussars Battle Group in Petrovec, Macedonia, debus as they train for operations in Kosovo.

Recce Platoon Scimitar.
'Cloughroe' with L/Sgt Fletcher and his section patrolling close to the Macedonia/Kosovo border, May 1999.

Even though mechanised, the Battalion still had to train on foot. No 1 Company preparing for operations in Kosovo at Petrovec, Macedonia.

L/Sgt David Brettle, alias 'Diamond Dave from Dudley', entertains the Kosovar Albanian children, Brazda, Macedonia. He played to audiences of up to 2,000 in the refugee camp, helping lift spirits in difficult circumstances.

Irish Guards Battle Group Headquarters finalising the plan, Petrovec, Macedonia, immediately before K-Day. *Clockwise round the table, from left:* Capt Michael Corbett, Intelligence Officer; Lt-Col Bill Cubitt, Commanding Officer; Major Michael Moriarty, Second in Command; Capt Peter McMullen, Operations Officer; Major Cassian Roberts, Battle Group Logistics Officer; Lt Mark Grayson, Signals Officer; Major Joe Fuller, Royal Engineers Squadron Commander; Major Paul Tilley, RA, 52 Battery Commander.

Right: **A final rendition of St Patrick's Day** by the Drums and Pipes on the morning of departure. L/Sgt Teague (flute); L/Cpl Gilfillan (Pipes); Piper Malone; Drummer Partington; Drummer McLoughlin (sitting on top); Gdsm Hughes (leaning on door).

Gdsm Estein ready to move.

A Warrior from No 1 Company, on K-Day+3 is greeted as it drives for the first time into Podujevo, Kosovo.

L/Cpl Beresford, Corps of Drums, finds use for a second helmet.

Pristina, 1999. The Commanding Officer, Lt-Col Bill Cubitt, negotiating with ethnic Albanians in Pristina. Note the 4th Armoured Brigade sign on his right sleeve.

Gdsm Ben Noble establishing good relations.

The Battalion remained in Kosovo for a further four months closely involved in Peace Keeping and helping the return to normality.

At the end of the Regiment's first one hundred years, the 1st Battalion Irish Guards are stationed at Münster in Germany.

APPENDIX A

The Colours

The Queen's Colour
1st Battalion – Gules (crimson): In the centre the Royal Cypher or, within the Collar of the Order of St Patrick with badge appendant proper, ensigned with The Crown.

The Regimental Colour
The Union, in the centre a company badge ensigned with The Crown. The 22 company badges are borne in rotation.

Battle Honours

The Battle Honours shown in heavy type below are borne upon the Queen's and Regimental Colour and on the Drums.

The Great War – Mons, **Retreat from Mons, Marne 1914, Aisne 1914, Ypres 1914, 17,** Langemarck 1914, Gheluvelt, Nonne Bosschen, **Festubert 1915, Loos, Somme, 1916, 18,** Fleurs Courcelette, Morval, Pilckem, Poelcappelle, Passchendaele, **Cambrai 1917, 18,** St Quentin, Lys, **Hazebrouck,** Albert 1918, Bapaume 1918, Arras 1918, Scarpe 1918, Drocourt-Queant, **Hindenburg Line,** Canal du Nord, Selle, Sambre, France and Flanders 1914–18.

The Second World War – Pothus, **Norway 1940, Boulogne 1940,** Cagny, **Mont Pincon, Neerpelt, Nijmegen,** Aalst, **Rhineland,** Hochwald, Rhine, Bentheim, **North-West Europe 1944–45,** Medjez Plain, **Djebel Bou Aoukaz 1943, North Africa 1943, Anzio,** Aprilia, Carroceto, Italy 1943–44.

Regimental Marches
Quick March – 'St Patrick's Day'
Slow March – 'Let Erin Remember'

Regimental Affiliations
4th Battalion The Royal Australian Regiment
The Royal Montserrat Defence Force
HMS *Boxer*

APPENDIX B

Victoria Cross

Citation No. 3556
Lance-Corporal Michael O'Leary
1 February 1915

'For conspicuous bravery at Cuinchy on the 1st February, 1915. When forming one of the storming party which advanced against the enemy's barricades he rushed to the front and himself killed five Germans who were holding the first barricade, after which he attacked a second barricade, about 60 yards further on, which he captured after killing three of the enemy and making prisoners of two more.

L/Cpl O'Leary thus practically captured the enemy's position by himself, and prevented the rest of the attacking party from being fired upon.'

Citation No. 7708
L/Sjt John Moyney
13 September 1917

'For most conspicuous bravery when in command of fifteen men forming two advanced posts. In spite of being surrounded by the enemy he held his post for ninety-six hours, having no water and little food. On the morning of the fifth day a large force of the enemy advanced to dislodge him. He ordered his men out of their shell-holes, and, taking the initiative, attacked with great effect from a flank. Finding himself surrounded by superior numbers, he led back his men in a charge through the enemy, and reached a stream which lay between the posts and the line. Here he instructed his party to cross at once while he and Pte Woodcock remained to cover their retirement.

When the whole of his force had gained the south-west bank unscathed he himself crossed under a shower of bombs. It was due to the endurance, skill and devotion to duty shown by this Non-Commissioned Officer that he was able to bring his entire force safely out of action.'

L/Cpl Michael O' Leary.

L/Sjt John Moyney.

Citation No. 8387
Pte Thomas Woodcock
Awarded 13 February 1917,
Gazetted 17 October 1917

'For most conspicuous bravery and determination. He was one of a post commanded by L/Sjt Moyney which was surrounded. The post held out for ninety-six hours, but after that time was attacked from all sides in overwhelming numbers and was forced to retire.

Pte Woodcock covered the retirement with a Lewis Gun, and only retired when the enemy had moved round and up to his post and were only a few yards away. He then crossed the river, but hearing cries for help behind him, returned and waded into the stream amid a shower of bombs from the enemy and rescued another member of the party. The latter he then carried across the open ground in broad daylight towards our front line regardless of machine-gun fire that was opened on him.'

Pte Thomas Woodcock.

Lt (acting Lt-Col) Neville Marshall VC, MC*
13 February 1919

'VC to Lt (acting Lt-Col) John Neville Marshall MC, late Irish Guards, Special Reserve, attached 16th Battalion, Lancashire Fusiliers: 'For most conspicuous bravery, determination and leadership in the attack on the Sambre-Oise Canal, near Catillon, on the 4th November 1918, when a partly constructed bridge came under concentrated fire and was broken before the advanced troops of his Battalion could cross. Lt-Col Marshall at once went forward and organised parties to repair the bridge.

The first party were soon killed or wounded, but by personal example he inspired and volunteers were instantly forthcoming. Under intense fire and with complete disregard of his own safety, he stood on the bank encouraging his men and assisting in the work, and when the bridge was repaired, attempted to rush across at the head of his Battalion and was killed while so doing.

The passage of the canal was of vital importance, and the gallantry displayed by all ranks was largely due to the inspiring example set by Lt-Col Marshall'

Lt, acting Lt-Col, Neville Marshall was a most unusual officer, a loner of strange character. He began the war in the Belgian Army (where his limited veterinary qualifications seem to have led to him being described, and probably employed as a military doctor). Wounded, and twice decorated by the Belgians for rescuing the wounded in November 1914, he was discharged and returned to England. He joined the Irish Guards with a chest full of ribbons from previous service. Without question he was gallant and very brave. His writings reveal a strange belief in destiny and a crusading zeal in which he likens himself to great figures in history. He was wounded many times, although the TEN wound stripes he wore after a wound in 1918 have yet to be authenticated. To his brother officers he was undoubtedly different. His age was open to question, there were stories about South Africa. Having won an MC and Bar with the Regiment, he was attached to the 16th Battalion The Lancashire Fusiliers to help boost the battalion which had suffered heavy losses. Such was his standing and reputation, he was soon appointed acting Commanding Officer. He was killed in an action of astounding bravery during the bounce crossing of the Sambre-Oise canal near Catillon (not far from Landrecies) on 4 November 1918. He was awarded a posthumous Victoria Cross, as was one of his company commanders. The War ended on 11 November.

Marshall's story is a strange one for he unquestionably was extraordinarily brave, and a very daring and experienced soldier. There is no question that he did not come from the same background as many of the officers, but equally, it is clear that this element was not, in those turbulent times, as important as it is often imagined to be. His competence and leadership were what mattered, and that was well proven in war. It does seem, however, that there was a reluctance in the Regiment to regard Marshall as a shining example. Perhaps Marshall curious Walter Mitty attitudes, his perceived vanity (extra ribbons and extra wound stripes) and his infatuation with his supposed historic destiny, may have (hardly surprisingly) somewhat alienated him from others of a less eccentric temperament. Couple this with his near reckless bravery and it becomes easier to understand how a Victoria Cross winner became to be regarded as so strange.

Lt Neville Marshall.

Citation No. 2722925
Lance-Corporal John Patrick Kenneally
1st Battalion
17 August 1943

'The Bou feature dominates all ground east and west between Medjez El Bab and Tebourba. It was essential to the final assault on Tunis that this feature should be captured and held.

A Guards Brigade assaulted and captured a portion of the Bou on 27 April 1943. The Irish Guards held on to points 212 and 214 on the western end of the feature, which points the Germans frequently counter-attacked. While a further attack to capture the complete feature was being prepared, it was essential for the Irish Guards to hold on. They did so.

On 28 April 1943, the positions held by one company of the Irish Guards on the ridge between points 212 and 214 were about to be subjected to an attack by the enemy. Approximately one company of the enemy were seen forming up preparatory to attack and L/Cpl Kenneally decided that this was the right moment to attack them himself. Single-handed he charged down the bare forward slope straight at the main enemy body, firing his Bren gun from the hip as he did so. This outstanding act of gallantry and the dash with which it was executed completely unbalanced the enemy company, which broke up in disorder. L/Cpl Kenneally then returned to the crest further to harass their retreat.

L/Cpl Kenneally repeated this remarkable exploit on the morning of 30 April 1943, when, accompanied by a sergeant of the Reconnaissance Corps, he again charged the enemy forming up for an assault. This time he so harassed the enemy, inflicting many casualties that this projected attack was frustrated. The enemy's strength was again about one company. It was only when he was noticed hopping from one fire position to another further to the left, in order to support another company, carrying his gun in one hand and supporting himself on a Guardsman with the other, that it was discovered that he had been wounded. He refused to give up his Bren gun, claiming that he was the only one who understood that gun, and continued to fight all through the day with great courage, devotion to duty and disregard for his own safety.

The magnificent gallantry of this NCO on these two occasions under heavy fire, his unfailing vigilance, and remarkable accuracy were responsible for saving many valuable lives during days and nights in the forward positions. His actions also played a considerable part in holding these positions and this influenced the whole course of the battle. His rapid appreciation of the situation, his initiative and his extraordinary gallantry in attacking single-handed a massed body of the enemy and breaking up an attack on two occasions, was an achievement that can seldom have been equalled. His courage in fighting all day when wounded was an inspiration to all ranks.'

L/Cpl John Patrick Kenneally.

Citation No. 2722614
Gdsm Edward Charlton
(posthumous), 6 February 1946

'On the morning of 21 April 1945, Gdsm Charlton was co-driver in one tank of a troop, which, with a Platoon of infantry seized the village of Wistedt.

Shortly afterwards, the enemy attacked this position under cover of an artillery concentration and in great strength, comprising as it later transpired, a Battalion of the 15th Panzer Grenadiers, supported by six self-propelled guns.

All the tanks, including Gdsm Charlton's, were hit; the infantry were hard pressed and in danger of being over-run.

Thereupon, entirely on his own initiative, Gdsm Charlton decided to counter-attack the enemy. Quickly recovering the Browning from his damaged tank, he advanced up the road in full view of the enemy, firing the Browning from his hip.

Such was the boldness of his attack and the intensity of his fire that he halted the leading enemy company, inflicting heavy casualties on them. This effort at the same time brought much needed relief to our own infantry.

For ten minutes Gdsm Charlton fired in his manner, until wounded in the left arm. Immediately, despite intense enemy fire, he mounted his machine-gun on a nearby fence which he used to support his wounded left arm. He stood firing thus for a further ten minutes until he was again hit in the left arm, which fell away shattered and useless.

Although twice wounded and suffering from loss of blood, Gdsm Charlton again lifted his machine-gun on to the fence, now having only one arm with which to fire and reload. Nevertheless, he still continued to inflict casualties on the enemy, until finally he was hit for a third time and collapsed. He died later of his wounds, in enemy hands. The heroism and determination of this Guardsman in his self-imposed task were beyond all praise. Even his German captors were amazed at his valour.

Gdsm Charlton's courageous and self-sacrificing action not only inflicted extremely heavy casualties on the enemy and retrieved his comrades from a desperate situation, but also enabled the position to be speedily recaptured.'

Gdsm Edward Charlton.

APPENDIX C

Casualties, Decorations and Battle Honours

THE GREAT WAR

- Strength before mobilization 1914: 997
- Borne on strength through the war: 293 Officers, 9,340 Other Ranks
- Killed in Action or died of wounds: 115 Officers, 2,235 Other Ranks
- Wounded: 148 Officers, approx. 5,000 Other Ranks
- Awards: 4 Victoria Cross, 14 Distinguished Service Order, 67 Military Cross, 77 Distinguished Conduct Medal, 244 Military Medal

THE SECOND WORLD WAR

Bn Theatre	Officers Killed/Died of Wounds	Officers Wounded	Other Ranks Killed/Died of Wounds	Other Ranks Wounded	Battalion Total	Total Casualties
1 Norway	7	5	13	23	48	
1 North Africa	9	16	115	229	369	
1 Italy	8	16	121	211	356	773
2 Hook of Holland	0	0	11	12	23	
2 Boulogne	2	1	23	14	40	
2 Normandy	7	15	51	96	169	
2 Belgium & Holland	3	18	54	100	175	
2 Germany	3	3	19	43	68	475
3 Normandy	7	6	67	182	262	
3 Belgium & Holland	7	28	143	413	591	
3 Germany	4	2	42	106	154	1007
Home	1	0	12	21	34	
Other	1	4	4	14	23	57
TOTAL	**59**	**114**	**675**	**1464**	**2312**	**2312**

Awards: 2 Victoria Cross, 17 Distinguished Service Order, 33 Military Cross, 18 Distinguished Conduct Medal, 72 Military Medal, 110 Mentioned in Despatches.

APPENDIX D

Colonels of the Regiment

Field Marshal the Rt Hon. The Earl Roberts of Kandahar and Pretoria and the City of Waterford
VC, KG, KP, PC, GCB, OM, GCSI, GCIE
17 October 1900 – 14 November 1914

Field Marshal The Rt Hon. The Earl Kitchener of Khartoum and of Broome KG, KP, PC, GCB, OM, GCSI, GCIE
15 November 1914 – 5 June 1916

Field Marshal The Earl of Ypres and High Lake KP, PC, GCB, OM, GCVO, KCMG, ADC
6 June 1916 – 22 May 1925

Field Marshal, The Earl of Cavan KP, GCB, GCMG, GCVO, GBE, DCL, LL.D, DL
23 May 1925 – 8 August 1946

Field Marshal The Rt Hon. The Earl Alexander of Tunis and Errigal in the County of Donegal KG, PC, GCB, OM, GCMG, CSI, DSO, MC, DCL, LL.D
28 August 1946 – 16 June 1969

General Sir Basil Eugster KCB, KCVO, CBE, DSO, MC*, MA
17 June 1969 – 5 April 1984

HRH, General The Grand Duke of Luxembourg KG
21 August 1984 –

APPENDIX E

Biographical Notes

General Sir Alexander Godley GCB, KCMG
Transferred to the Irish Guards in 1900. Major-General Imperial General Staff and GOC New Zealand Forces (1910–14); Divisional and Corps Commander Dardanelles and Egypt (1914–16); Commander Army Corps (1916–19); Military Secretary (1920–22); C in C British Army of the Rhine (1922–24); GOC in C Southern Command (1924–28); Governor and C in C Gibraltar (1928–33)

Field Marshal The Rt Hon. The Earl Alexander of Tunis and Errigal in the County of Donegal KG, PC, GCB, OM, GCMG, CSI, DSO, MC
Commanded 2nd Battalion (1917–18); Baltic Landeswehr (1920–21); 1st Battalion (1922–26); Regimental Lieutenant-Colonel (1928–30); Nowshera Brigade, Northwest Frontier (1934–38); 1st Division (1938–40); 1st Corps (1940); Southern Command (1940–42); Burma (1942); Middle East and 18th Army Group (1942–43), Allied Armies, Italy (1943–44); Allied Commander Mediterranean (1944–45); Governor General of Canada (1946–52); Minister of Defence (1952–54); Constable of HM Tower of London (1960–65)

Major-General Charles Haydon CB, DSO*, OBE
Commanded 2nd Battalion 1940. Raised Special Service Brigade (forerunner of the Commandos) and commanded them in the Vaagso Raid in Norway (1943) and that on the Lofoten Islands (1943); Vice Chief Combined Operations (to Lord Louis Mountbatten); Commanded 1st Guards Brigade (1944); British Joint Services Mission, Washington (1944–45); Chief, Intelligence Division Control Commission, Germany (1945–47)

Major-General Gerald Verney DSO, MVO
Commanded 2nd Battalion (1940–42); 32nd Guards
Brigade (1942); 6th Guards Tank Brigade (1942–44); 7th
Armoured Division (1944); 1st Guards Brigade (1945);
Commander Vienna Area (1945–46); 56th (London)
Armoured Division (TA) (1946–48)

General Sir Basil Eugster KCB, KCVO, CBE, DSO, MC*
Commanded 3rd Battalion (1945); 2nd Battalion (1947);
1st Battalion (1951–54); Commandant Mons Officer
Cadet School (1958); 3rd Infantry Brigade (1959–62);
Commandant School of Infantry, Warminster (1962–63);
GOC 4th Division, BAOR (1963–65); GOC London
District and Major-General Commanding the Household
Brigade (1965–68); Commander British Forces Hong
Kong (1968–70); GOC in C Southern Command
(1971–72); C in C United Kingdom Land Forces (1972–74)

Major-General Sir Robert Corbett KCVO, CB
Commanded 1st Battalion (1981–84); Chief of Staff
British Forces Falkland Islands (1984–85); 6th Airborne
Brigade (1985–87); Director Defence Programmes,
Ministry of Defence (1987–88); GOC Berlin (British
Sector) and British Commandant (1989–91); Regimental
Lieutenant Colonel (1988–91); GOC London District and
Major-General Commanding the Household Division
(1991–94).

APPENDIX F

Bibliography

Rudyard Kipling, *The Irish Guards in the Great War, The First Battalion*, 1923 (reprinted 1997 by Spellmount Publishers)

Rudyard Kipling, *The Irish Guards in the Great War, The Second Battalion*, 1923 (reprinted 1997 by Spellmount Publishers)

Desmond FitzGerald, *A History of the Irish Guards in the Second World War*, 1949

Peter Verney, *The Micks: The Story of the Irish Guards*, Peter Davies, 1970

Capt 'Tinker' Taylor MC **and Capt Sandy Faris,** *The Armoured Micks 1941–45: The Story of the 2nd Battalion Irish Guards*, 1997

APPENDIX G

Glossary

120mm	120mm BAT, MOBAT or WOMBAT, all versions of a large recoilless infantry anti-tank weapon
2IC	Second in Command. Until 1918 the Irish Guards referred to the Senior Major in the Grenadier fashion (a reflection of the origins of many of the important early opinion formers in the Irish Guards)
2/Lt	Second Lieutenant (referred to as an Ensign)
66mm	66mm Disposable anti-tank launcher
81mm	81mm Mortar, replaced the 3 inch mortar in 1962
84mm	84mm Carl Gustav shoulder held recoilless anti-tank weapon
ACC	Army Catering Corps
ADC	Aide de Camp. Personal staff officer of a General
AFV	Armoured Fighting Vehicle, followed by a 3 figure identification
APC	Armoured Personnel Carrier
ARU	Annual review of a unit
ASM	Artificer Sergeant Major
AT	Animal Transport
Atk	Anti-tank
BATUS	British Army Training Unit Suffield (Alberta, Canada)
BEM	British Empire Medal
Bn	Battalion
Brig	Brigadier (formerly Brigadier General)
C/Sgt	Colour Sergeant
C/Sjt	Colour Serjeant (pre-1914)
Capt	Captain
CBE	Commander of the British Empire
CIE	Commander of the Indian Empire
Col	Colonel. Rank of the Regimental Lieutenant Colonel. (He holds (tenant) the place (lieu) of the Colonel of the Regiment.)
Coy	Company (abbreviated to avoid confusion with CO, shorthand for the Commanding Officer outside the Household Division)
CQMS	Company Quartermaster Sergeant
CSM	Company Sergeant Major (Warrant Officer Class 2)
CSMIM	Company Sergeant Major Instructor in Musketry
CVO	Commander of the Royal Victorian Order
D/Sgt	Drill Sergeant (Warrant Officer Class 2)
D/Sjt	Drill Serjeant, pre-1914 a Colour Sergeant, later a WO2
DCM	Distinguished Conduct Medal. The highest award next to the Victoria Cross available until 1995 to Warrant and Non Commissioned Officers and Guardsmen. Many were disappointed when this highly respected medal was discontinued in 1996
DF	Defensive fire
DMS	Directly Moulded Sole (replacement for the ammunition boot)
DPM	Disruptive Pattern Material
DSO	Distinguished Service Order
FM	Field Marshal
GCB	Knight Grand Cross of the Bath
GCIE	Knight Grand Cross of the Indian Empire
GCSI	Knight Grand Cross of the Star of India
Gdsm	Guardsman
GOC	General Officer Commanding
GOC in C	General Officer Commanding in Chief
GPMG	General Purpose Machine-Gun
Gren Gds	Grenadier Guards
HQ	Headquarters
KG	Knight of the Garter
KIA	Killed in Action
KP	Knight of St Patrick
L/Cpl	Lance Corporal
L/Sgt	Lance Sergeant
L/Sjt	Lance Serjeant (pre-1914)
LAD	Light Aid Detachment
Lt	Lieutenant
Lt-Col	Lieutenant Colonel. Rank of the Commanding officer of a Battalion

Maj	Major
MBE	Member of the Order of the British Empire
MC	Military Cross, awarded to officers from January 1915 to 1996, and then broadened to include all ranks. It will be noted that some of the pre-1916 DCM awards would probably later have been MMs. This was a contributory reason for its introduction
MILAN	French Infantry Anti -Tank missile system which superceded the WOMBAT in the 1980s
MM	Military Medal, introduced 25 March 1916 and awarded to Warrant and Non Commissioned Officers and Guardsmen for Bravery in the Field. Discontinued in 1996
MT	Motor Transport
MVO	Member of the Victorian Order
NCO	Non Commissioned Officer
OP	Observation Post
Op	Operation
P/Sgt	Pay Sergeant (a Grenadier expression for the CQMS, which the Irish Guards originally adopted, but dropped during the Great War)
PIAT	Projectile Infantry Anti-Tank. A Second World War vintage weapon
PSM	Platoon Sergeant Major (Warrant Officer Class 3)
Pte	Private soldier (replaced by Guardsman in the Foot Guards by The King's command in 1919)
QM	Quartermaster
RAF	Royal Air Force
REME	Royal Electrical and Mechanical Engineers
RIC	Royal Irish Constabulary
RQMS	Regimental Quartermaster Sergeant
RSM	Regimental Sergeant Major (the senior Warrant Officer of the Battalion)
RTR	Royal Tank Regiment
SA 80	Small Arms 80. The rifle and light assault weapon which succeeded the SLR in the early 1980s
SF	Sustained fire (GPMG)
Sgt	Sergeant (or Full Sergeant)
Sjt	Serjeant. As spelled in the Brigade of Guards before the Great War
SLR	Self Loading Rifle, 7.62mm calibre. Based on the Belgian FN it superceded the Lee Enfield No 4 Rifle in 1959
Swingfire	Anti-tank missile system fired from AFV 438 to a range in excess of 4,000 metres
Temp	Temporary
TQMS	Technical Quartermaster
VC	Victoria Cross
WIA	Wounded in Action
WO1	Warrant Officer Class 1
WO2	Warrant Officer Class 2

APPENDIX H

Acknowledgements

The Regiment owes an immense debt for the creation of this book to Colonel Sir William Mahon Bt and his Committee – Pat Bowen; Major Tony Brady, the Regimental Archivist, whose background sleuthing was invaluable; Lt-Col Robin Bullock-Webster OBE; Major Brian Gilbart-Denham; Major John Lockwood; The Lord Monteagle of Brandon; Brigadier Mick O'Cock CBE, MC; Lt-Col Brian O'Gorman; Lt-Col James Pollock MBE; Major Peter Verney and Sir Anthony Weldon Bt, who presided over the technical production and Brigadier Christopher Wolverson, Regimental Lieutenant Colonel.

Also to the very many Micks and ex-Micks who have helped by giving their time, their advice and in many instances lending their photographs. In particular Martin Aldridge, a number of whose excellent pictures adorn these pages, and Fergus Greer, a professional photographer, who was invited to accompany the 1st Battalion into Kosovo and whose portrayal of this exciting event in the Regiment's history concludes this book. Don Kearney, who kindly lent from his own collection the poster on the back cover. Capt 'Tinker' Taylor MC and former members of the 2nd Battalion who have also helped unravel the complexities of the tank.

INDEX